W9-DFN-865

BASIC TERMS OF SHINTO

compiled by
Shinto Committee
for the
IXth International Congress
for the
History of Religions

JINJA HONCHO (THE ASSOCIATION OF SHINTO SHRINES)
KOKUGAKUIN UNIVERSITY
INSTITUTE FOR JAPANESE CULTURE AND CLASSICS

1958, Tokyo

PREFACE

This booklet is a brief exposition of selective terms of Shinto. This is compiled for the convenience of historians of religions who have gathered to attend the IXth International Congress for the History of Religions.

Shinto is a religion developed indigenously in the Japanese soil. So it is unique in many ways, its doctorinal formation and forms of rites and festivals. There are a good many words of Shinto which could not be adequately translated into European languages. Precise understanding of them would be invaluable help for the inquiry of religious life of the Japanese people. We shall be happy if this booklet is of any use to visitors who wish to study Shinto and observe the Shinto shrines.

Shinto Committee for the
IXth International Congress
for the History of Religions

CONTRIBUTORS

Motohiko ANZU	:	Dr., Professor, Kokugakuin University.
Hirobumi GÔDA	:	Research Fellow, Institute for Japanese Culture and Classics, Kokugakuin University.
Naofusa HIRAI	:	Associate Professor, Kokugakuin University.
Tokuichi IWAMOTO	:	Professor, Kokugakuin University.
Junichi KAMATA	:	Research Fellow, Institute for Japanese Culture and Classics, Kokugakuin University.
Harukuni MIYAJI	:	Research Fellow, Institute for Japanese Culture and Classics, Kokugakuin University.
Masayoshi NISHITSUNOI	:	Dr., Professor, Kokugakuin University.
Haruo OGASAWARA	:	Research Fellow, Institute for Japanese Culture and Classics, Kokugakuin University.
Yoneo OKADA	:	Head of the Research Division, The Association of Shinto Shrines.
Kazuteru ONO	:	Research Assistant, Kokugakuin University.
Motonori ONO	:	Dr., Professor, Kokugakuin University.
Jingoro USUDA	:	Professor, Kokugakuin University.

MEMBERS OF THE SHINTO COMMITTEE FOR THE IXth INTERNATIONAL CONGRESS FOR THE HISTORY OF RELIGIONS

Nobusuke TAKATSUKASA	:	President, The Association of Shinto Shrines.
Yasuji AKIOKA	:	Director-General, The Association of Shinto Shrines.
Arata FURUYA	:	Managing Director, The Association of Shinto Shrines.
Yayoi MOTOORI	:	Accountant General and Head of Secretarial Division, The Association of Shinto Shrines.
Iwakichi ISHIKAWA	:	President, Kokugakuin University.
Saburo MATSUO	:	Managing Director, Kokugakuin University.
Takeji KOBAYASHI	:	Managing Director, Kokugakuin University.
Kiyoshi TANAKA	:	Managing Director, Kokugakuin University.
Michio YOSHIDA	:	Head of the General Affairs Section, Kokugakuin University.
*Motohiko ANZU	:	Professor, Kokugakuin University.
*Naofusa HIRAI	:	Associate Professor, Kokugakuin University.
*Ichiro HORI	:	Professor, Kokugakuin University.
*Tokuichi IWAMOTO	:	Professor, Kokugakuin University.
*Harukuni MIYAJI	:	Research Fellow, Institute for Japanese Culture and Classics, Kokugakuin University.
**Masayoshi NISHITSUNOI	:	Professor, Kokugakuin University.
*Motonori ONO	:	Professor, Kokugakuin University.
*Yoneo OKADA	:	Head of the Research Division, The Association of Shinto Shrines.
*Mitsumasa SHOMOTO	:	Head of the Educational Division, The Association of Shinto Shrines.
*Yoshio TODA	:	Associate Professor, Kokugakuin University.
*Jingoro USUDA	:	Professor, Kokugakuin University.

(*···Member of the Executive Committee, **····Chairman of the Executive Committee)

ITEMIZED LIST OF TRANSLATED TERMS

英 訳 分 類 項 目 表

I. General Terms

Shintô, 62
Shrine Shintô, 24
State Shintô, 33
Unity of government and religion → *Kokka Shintô*
Imperial Way → *Kokka Shintô*
Religious ceremonies of the Imperial House, 34
Folk beliefs, 40
Sectarian Shintô, 36

Syncretism of Shintô and Buddhism, 56
Honji Suijaku theory, 17
Ryôbu Shintô, 48
Shingon Shintô, 58
Ryôbu Shûgô Shintô → *Shingon Shintô*
Tendai Shintô, 70
Sannô Ichijitsu Shintô → *Tendai Shintô*
Ise Shintô, 19
Watarai Shintô → *Ise Shintô*
Yoshida Shintô, 80
Mito-gaku, 41
Suiga Shintô, 65
Fukko Shintô, 9
Separation of Shintô and Buddhism, 56
"Heart Learning", 57
Popular Shintô, 75

Sacred books of Shintô, 61
Kojiki, 32
Nihon Shoki, 43
Nihongi → *Nihon Shoki*
Fudoki, 9
Manyôshû, 37
Ritsu, 48
Ryô, 48
Engi-shiki, 9
Kogo Shûi, 32
Shinsen Shôji-roku, 60
Sendai Kuji Hongi, 52
Shintô Go-bu-sho, 63
Sanja Takusen, 50

Dajô-kan, 6
Jingi-kan, 21
Bureau of Shintô Shrines, 23
Shrine Board, 21
Kokugakuin University, 33
Jingû Kôgaku-kan, 22
Association of Shintô Shrines, 23

Yoshida, Kanetomo, 80
Watarai (Deguchi), Nobuyoshi, 77
Yamazaki, Ansai, 79
Kada no Azuma-maro, 25
Kamo no Mabuchi, 28
Motoori, Norinaga, 41
Hirata, Atsutane, 16

II. Theoretical Field

Theology, 57
Kan-nagara no michi → *Kan-nagara*
Musubi, 42
Heaven and earth, 1
Plain of High Heaven, 68
Perpetual Country, 72
Abundant Reed-plain Land, Japan, 74
This world, 76
Subterranean world, 43
Land of Gloom, 79
Invisible world, 27

Kami, 27, 71, 1
Deities → *Kami*
Mikoto, 39
Divine virtue, 63
Divine dignity, 38

III. Deities

IV. Shinto Shrine

V. Ceremonies and Festivals

VI. Priests and Other Religious Leaders

VII. Religious Groups

VIII. Miscellany

LIST OF TERMS IN ALPHABETICAL ORDER

アルファベット順項目表

A.

B.

C.

D.

E.

F.

G.

M.

N.

O.

R.

S.

T.

U.

LIST OF ILLUSTRATIONS

Ai-dono : In cases when several deities are enshrined in the same *Honden** of a shrine, the principal deity is enshrined in the center, and the altars to the left and right are used to enshrine the subordinate deities. These subordinate altars are called *ai-dono,* and the deities abiding upon them are called *ai-dono-no-kami.*

Akaku kiyoki kokoro : ⟶ Seimei.

Akimatsuri : A festival celebrated in autumn. The antithesis of the spring festival, the autumn festival is one thanking the gods for an abundant harvest. As the name of the month *kan-na-zuki* ("godless month") reveals, this festival was anciently preceded by one month of strict taboo. Many of the annual festivals of the shrines possess the characteristics of autumn festivals. *Niiname-sai* is a festival celebrated November 23–24 when the Emperor offers the first-fruits of the year's grain harvest and himself partakes thereof. *Kanname-sai* is a festival of the Grand Shrine of Ise when the first-fruits are offered to the Goddess; in the Gekû it is celebrated on October 15–16, and in the Naikû on October 16–17.

Aku : Evil. Not only evil in the moral sense, also means unhappiness, disaster, inferiority of the nature or value of a thing. See also *tsumi, kegare, hito.*

Ama-terasu-ô-mikami : Also known by the name Ô-hiru-me-no-muchi. The ancestral deity of the Imperial House. A goddess endowed with the virtue of the sun's rays. The one of his offspring most beloved by Izanagi-no-mikoto, a goddess of a most refined and gentle disposition. The goddess embodying the unity of *Takama no Hara,** who also showed man the way of making food, clothing, and dwellings; the goddess who is the basis of peace. She dispatched her grandson Ninigi to the land *Toyo-ashi-hara no naka-tsu-kuni* to become the embodiment of its unification, and to cause his descendants to be the Imperial House. Ise Jingū is the shrine which worships this great goddess, by means of the *Yata* Mirror (see *Sanshu no Shinki*) which she bestowed. There are many shrines throughout the country where she is enshrined.

Ama-tsu-kami, Kuni-tsu-kami : ⟶ Kami.

Ame no masu-hito : ⟶ Hito.

Ame-no-minakanushi-no-kami : ⟶ Musubi.

Ame-tsuchi : *Ame* means heaven, and *tsuchi* means earth. In Shinto, *ame* is sacred, while *tsuchi* is lowly. There is a myth which explains that, at the time of the creation, the light, pure elements branched off to become *ame*, and the heavy, turbid elements branched off and became *tsuchi*. Consequently, *ame* is the home and dwelling place of the sacred gods, the *Ama-tsu-kami* (Gods of Heaven); while *tsuchi* is the dwelling place of the gods living on the earth, the spirit-gods called *kuni-tsu-kami* (Gods of the Land). It is for this reason that the Shinto mythology speaks of the *Ama-tsu-kami* descending from Heaven to pacify and perfect this world.

Ao-hito-gusa : ⟶ Hito.

Aoi matsuri.

Aoi matsuri : An annual festival celebrated every year on May 15 at the two Kamo shrines in Kyôto. Said to have originated in the region of Emperor Kimmei, around 1400 years ago, as a festival to pray for abundant grain harvests. On the festival day, a dignified procession in costumes sets out from the Kyôto Palace and goes through the city towards the shrines. There are ox-drawn carts, golden saddles on the horses, and hollyhock (*aoi*) flowers displayed on the head-dresses of all the participants. This festival, presenting a veritable scroll of impressive scenes, is one of the three biggest festivals in Japan.

Araburu kami : Malignant gods who bring affliction to man. Although they do not really deserve to be considered as *kami*,* in Shinto it has been thought possible to soothe and pacify their evil hearts and actions by *matsuri** and thus change them into benevolent deities.

Aramitama, Nigimitama : ⟶ Tama.

Asa-gutsu : A kind of *kutsu* (shoe). Evidently was originally of leather, but since the Heian period has consisted of hollowed paulownia wood painted on the outside with black lacquer. Used at all times by ancient nobles. Today is the footgear worn by Shinto priests during religious ceremonies.

Asa-gutsu.

Azuma-asobi: Literally, "music and dancing of the Eastern countries." The ancient inhabitants of the Eastern provinces, towards whose loyalty anxiety was felt, offered their music as a token of their submission to the Court. During the reign of Emperor Daigo, the musical notation of the songs of the *Azuma-asobi* was fixed by Imperial command. It was largely songs from the regions Sagami and Suruga which were included. Today still performed in the Court and in shrines.

Bachi: The retribution given by a god to someone who has performed words or actions of disrespect, disbelief, or impurity towards a god. *Bachi* is a corruption of the sound of the Chinese character *batsu*, meaning punishment.

Bekka: ⟶ Saikai.

Beppyô jinja: Literally, "Shrines on the Separate List." From all the shrines in the country, the former national or state shrines and other large shrines were listed by the Jinja Honchô in a special list in order to facilitate work. A special term in shrine administration. At present 244 have been selected.

Bokusen: Divination. From antiquity there have been many means of determining the good or ill fortune of a thing or undertaking and ascertaining the divine will with regard to a matter. Besides the *futo-mani,* which consisted of firing the shoulder plate of a deer and divining by the resulting cracks, and *kiboku,* which consisted of firing the shell of a tortoise, there were a good many forms of divination.

Bon-matsuri: A festival celebrated around July 15 in order to console the spirits of the dead. On the 13th, a fire called *mukae-bi* (welcoming fire) is burned at the entrance of each house; by this the spirits of the dead are welcomed into the house and offerings are made to them on the altar. On the 15th, another fire called *okuri-bi* (sending-off fire) is burned to send off the spirits on their return. Or there are some places where, instead of the *okuri-bi,* lanterns are floated down a river. This festival is said to originate in Buddhism; but it is clear that it is based on native beliefs antecedent to Buddhism and that Buddhist practices were later added to these native customes.

Bugaku (Ceremonial music and dancing).

Bugaku : Ceremonial music and dancing. Synonymous with *gagaku*;* yet *bugaku* is always accompanied with sacred dancing.

Chien-shin : A deity worshipped by a natural group living in a definite area. In the broad sense, can include a part of *uji-gami** and *ubusuna-no-kami,** but usually refers to the village god, a deity worshipped by a smaller geographical group than those worshipping an *uji-gami* or *ubusuna-no-kami.* There are cases where a *ketsuen-shin** or a *dôzoku-shin** has become a *chien-shin,* or where deities of other localities have been introduced as *chien-shin* of new localities. The *chien-shin* is chiefly a deity protecting the region in which worshipped, but since the Meiji period there are many cases of the *chien-shin* of small groups being incorporated in the *uji-gami.*

Chigi, katsuogi.

Chigi, katsuogi : The crossed beams sticking up on both ends of the gable boards or the roof in Shinto architecture are called *chigi.* Also the boards which stand up on the roof at right angles to the ridge of the roof are called *katsuogi.* Both are remnants of ancient architecture.

Chinju-no-kami : A tutelary god protecting a definite area. In some cases confused with *uji-gami* or *ubusuna-no-kami.** When a person settles of builds a building in a certain place, he performs a *jichin-sai,** a celebration in honor of the spirit dwelling already in the place; or else he invites from elsewhere a god in order to have the god protect the place forever. The *chinju-no-kami* exist in the Imperial capital, in large mansions, in Buddhist temples, and in the territories and castles of lordly families; and these deities came gradually to be worshipped as *uji-gami** or *ubusuna-no-kami*.

Chinkon : ⟶ Tama.

Chi-no-wa : A type of implement used in casting out mishap. It is a large sacred ring made of loosely twisted miscanthus reeds; exorcism is accomplished by passing the body through this large loop. This ancient ceremony is practiced everywhere on the festival of *O-harae** on June 30.

Chi-no-wa.

Chokusai : A festival celebrated in the presence of a *chokushi* (Imperial Messenger) specially dispatched by the Imperor. Besides the Grand Shrine of Ise, over ten shrines, including the two Kamo shrines, the Iwashimizu Hachiman-gû, Meiji Jingû, etc., possess this status, and these shrines are called *chokusai-sha*.

Chokusai-sha : ⟶ Chokusai.

Chokushi : Imperial messenger. A messenger dispatched to convey the greetings of the Imperor on the occasion of a shrine festival. *Chokushi* are dispatched to the three great festivals of Ise Jingû—the *Toshi-goi,** *Kanname* and *Niiname* festivals—the annual festivals of *chokusai-sha** such as the two Kamo shrines in Kyôto, etc.

Chûsai : ⟶ Taisai.

Da-gakki : The percussion instruments used in Gagaku are collectively called *sanko* (three drums), or *uchi-mono* (striking instruments), and include the *taiko, kakko,* and *shôko.*

Dai-gûji: In ordinary shrines, the chief priest is called *gûji;* but in the Ise Jingû the post of the priest who assists the *saishu,** participates in religious ceremonies, and supervises all business, is called *Dai-gûji,* or Supreme Priest.

Daijô-sai: A great festival when the newly crowned Emperor offers, for the first time in his reign, the first-fruits to Ama-terasu-ô-mikami* and the other gods. In its significance it does not differ from the *Niiname-sai,** but differs in that it is celebrated at the beginning of a new reign. By performing this festival, the Emperor becomes truly an Emperor in fact as well as in name.

Daikoku: The Indian deity Mahâkâla. In Japan the belief in this deity became general in the middle ages together with the belief in the deity Ebisu, and Daikoku was combined with the native deity Ô-kuni-nushi-no-kami. At first this deity was the god of the kitchen, but later came to be worshipped as the god of happiness, and in Western Japan, combined with the god of the rice-fields (*ta-no-kami**), is worshipped as the god of agricultural cultivation.

Daikoku.

Dajô-kan: Name of a government office in the *ritsu-ryô* system (seventh to ninth centuries) in charge of all political affairs and local administration. Founded in emulation of the system of T'ang China. Together with the *Jingi-kan,** was one of the two highest government offices. At the Meiji Restoration, the *Dajô-kan* was restored and made the highest government office on July 8, 1869; but the office was abolished on December 22, 1885.

Dashi: A car drawn at festivals. In various regions called *yama-boko,* hiki-yama, mai-guruma, odori-guruma, yatai,* etc. Shaped like a mountain, a shrine, a boat, etc. Either drawn by a vehicle or borne on the shoulders by a multitude. A pole (*hoko*) is raised high in the center, dolls are displayed, and paper lanterns are lit all over the car. They are beautifully decorated, and are moved to the accompaniment of festive music. One of the styles of greeting a deity at a ceremonial place; ancient in origin, it developed in recent times.

Dashi (Float).

Dengaku: A musical performance originating in rice planting ceremonies. Accompanied by the music of flutes, drums, and wooden blocks called *sasara*, the *sa-otome* (rice-planting maidens) would plant the young rice shoots while singing songs. Toward the middle of the Heian period, the inhabitants of Kyôto also came to enjoy this performance, which was taken into the festivals of shrines. Later professional musicians called *dengaku-hôshi* appeared, and *dengaku* became commercialized, but in the Muromachi period died out, overwhelmed by the popularity of *Sarugaku Nô.* Today is performed at the festivals of Asakusa Jinja in Tôkyô and Nachi Jinja in Wakayama Prefecture.

Dôsojin.

Dôsojin: A deity, called also *Sai-no-kami* or *Dôroku-jin,* worshipped on the village borders, or on mountain passes, cross-roads, or by bridges, in order to keep away pestilent spirits or demons coming from without. Also worshipped as the god of roads and travel and attributed with various characteristics. As a result of the syncretism with Buddhism, there is a widespread custom of erecting stone images of Jizô.

Dôzoku-shin: "Kinship deity"; a deity of a family group unified in the consciousness of possessing a common paternal ancestry (a family group actually living together in the same village and having a real genealogical relation). There are cases of worshipping the ancestor of the family group and of worshipping a deity introduced from elsewhere; but in either case the worship of ancestral spirits seems to be at the background. Important, together with the belief in the *ujigami,** as a means of knowing the fundamental religious forms of the Japanese people. Usually the *honke* or original house (from which the other houses may have branched off) is entrusted with carrying out the worship, and at the festival the entire kinship group assembles; by performing a festival in common, they strengthen the solidarity of the group and simultaneously pray for its prosperity. The belief in *dôzoku-shin* in Japan presents many complex facets.

Ebisu.

Ebisu : A deity thought to protect the necessary livelihoods and to impart happiness and prosperity; generally regarded as one with the native deity Koto-shiro-nushi-no-kami. Ebisu is worshipped in the cities as the god of merchants and in the country villages as the god of the rice-fields (*ta no kami*),* but these beliefs were derived from the fishing villages, where Ebisu is both thought of as the god of abundant catches and believed to have appeared from out of the sea, to be a god from a far country; here the idea of receiving blessings from a deity from a far country is strong.

Eboshi : Headgear for Shintô priests. Used in case they are in abbreviated costume, such as *kariginu** or *jôe.**

Eboshi.

Ema : Votive pictures presented to shrines; in the practice of hanging paintings of horses in front of the deity as a substitute for making a votive offering of sacred horses. Gradually variety increased in the form and style of the paintings, and works of the most famous artists of the age began to appear. In some shrines, there are special buildings, called *ema-den,* where these pictures are displayed.

E-maki-mono : Picture scrolls; refers to scrolls containing both paintings and their explanations. Unique to Japan, this art form flourished after the Heian period. This method was used to depict the foundation and wonders of shrines; the national treasure "Kitano Tenjin Engi" possessed by Kitano Tenman-gû in Kyôto is particularly famous.

Engi-shiki: A collection of minute regulations about government administration current during the period of *ritsu-ryô* law (7th until late 9th century). The *Engi-shiki* was a compilation in 50 volumes formulated with consideration of the two preceding compilations, the *Kônin* and *Jôgan* compilations; of these three large compilations, the *Engi-shiki* is the only one still extant today. It is a compilation of Court laws defining in detail Imperial Court ceremonies and etiquette, expediential measures, local administration, etc. Compilation was begun in 905 AD, and the completed work was presented at Court in 927, but it was not actually promulgated until 967. It was compiled by Fujiwara Tokihira, Fujiwara Tadahira, and others. The first ten volumes are regulations concerning Shinto, and are especially highly valued as a treasure trove for the study of Shinto ritual.

Ennichi.

Ennichi: A day on which believers go to visit the shrine of the deity they believe in. It is believed that merit is gained by visiting on a particular day each month; the custom also is common in Buddhism. Because of the large crowds of people who visit the shrine on these days, markets sprang up to sell commodities, and there were settlements which grew up around the shrines and temples.

Fudoki: Works of local geography presented to the Court in response to an Imperial order in 713 A.D. to the local governments to record and present to the Court information on the origin of geographical names, the fertility of the soil, the products, and the old tales and legends of the local regions. At present most of them are lost, but the complete book of the *Izumo Fudoki,* and fragments of the *Hitachi, Harima, Bungo,* and *Hizen Fudoki.* There are also works of local geography compiled in the Tokugawa period using the same name.

Fukko Shinto: Literally, "Restoration Shinto," "Reform Shinto." One of the Shinto schools. Kada no Azumamaro* (1669–1736 AD), Kamo no Mabuchi* (1697–1769 AD), Motoori Norinaga* (1730–1801 AD), and Hirata Atsutane* (1776–1843 AD) belonged to it. The object of the other Shinto schools was the re-discovery of ancient, natural Shinto, but most of them relied in their research on Buddhist or Confucian methodology or ways of thought and therefore as a result gave birth to Buddhistic or Confucianistic theories of Shinto. However, this school of *Fukko Shintô,* beginning from a painstaking study of ancient philology, attempted to make clear the mentality of the ancient Japanese and thus to discover the essence of Shinto. Consequently, in its accomplishments there are many things which stand comparison with present-day learning; in this sense, this school was epoch-making in the history of Shinto studies.

Funa-dama : A spirit worshipped by fishermen and seafarers as the deity protecting ships. A hole is made in the mast of the ship and women's hair, dolls, two dice, twelve pieces of money, and the five grains are put in and regarded as the symbol of the spirit. Widely believed to be a goddess, and also believed to grant abundant catches when worshipped at times when catches are poor.

Funa-dama.

Funa-kurabe : Boat races between villages; strong men are chosen from each of the contesting villages. Frequently held in the festivals of regions on the shores of Western Japan. Originally had the significance of divining whether the year's harvest would be plentiful. Also held at Iki, Tsushima, and Sakura-jima. The famous *peiron* of Nagasaki is also an example of this.

Funa-kurabe. (Boat races).

Gagaku : Ceremonial music and dancing handed down from antiquity in the Imperial Court and still preserved today in the Music Department of the Imperial Household and in famous shrines and temples. Naturally, Gagaku also contains many elements which were handed down from China and India. With the accompaniment of reed instruments and percussion instruments, it is performed by dancers wearing the prescribed costumes and masks and holding prescribed objects in their hands. Instrumental music having no accompanying dancing is simply called *kangen,* and that with dancing is called *Bugaku.** There are many pieces, such as Ranryôô, Nasori, Gejôraku, etc.

Gaku : ⟶ Ema.

Gakubu : Special department where the traditional, sacred music and dancing are performed; belongs in the Board of Ceremonies, Imperial Household.

Gense : ⟶ Utsushi-yo.

Gion : Refers to the gods, chiefly Susa-no-o-no-mikoto,* enshrined in the Yasaka Jinja in Kyôto City. Worshipped as a deity able to cast out and purify all evils. Anciently was known as *Gion-sha.* The shrine's festival, the *Gion-e* (July 17–24), is historically famous and is one of the three biggest festivals in Japan.

Gion matsuri : A festival celebrated every year from July 17 to 24 at the Yasaka Jinja in Kyôto. Said to have originated around 1100 years ago, during the reign of Emperor Seiwa, as a festival to guard against pestilence. Today the procession of the *yama-boko** floats through the city on the 17th and 24th is the climax of the festival. These floats, displaying dolls and sculptures created by the hands of the greatest artists and even Gobelin tapestries imported from abroad, are in themselves precious as cultural treasures.

Gishiki-den : A shrine building used for performing special rites and ceremonies. As a rule, shrine ceremonies are performed in the *Heiden** or *Haiden**; cut besides these, in recent years special ceremonies such as weddings performed in accordance with the demands of the faithful have increased greatly, and there are many shrines which have established special buildings to deal with these.

Go-bunrei : Literally, "divided spirit." Frequently a branch of a shrine is established; in this case, the practice of dividing the spirit of the deity of the former shrine, as well as the divided spirit are called *go-bunrei.*

Go-hei : A type of *heihaku;* paper or cloth offered to a god and attached to a stick. Believed originally to have been a method of presenting offerings of cloth. But with the development of paper and under the influence of knowledge of the *Yin-yang* philosophy, there came to be various styles. There is also a viewpoint regarding it as the *mi-tama-shiro** of the deity.

Go-hei.

Gon-gen: As a result of the syncretism of Buddhism and Shinto, the concept that a Buddha of India came to appear in Japan in the form of a Shinto *kami** in order to save the Japanese was developed, and the term *gongen,* applied to this type of god, came to be widely used. Consequently the term *gongen* was generally applied to the names of previously known deities.

Gongen-zukuri: A style of shrine architecture. One of the oldest examples is the Kitano Tenman-gû shrine of Kyôto. Usually consists of three buildings, the *Honden,* Heiden,** and *Haiden,** joined together in an H shape. Flourished after of the Momoyama period.

Gon-gûji: ⟶ Shinshoku.

Gon-negi: ⟶ Shinshoku.

Go-shintai: ⟶ Shintai.

Gûji: ⟶ Shinshoku.

Hachiman: Generally refers to the three deities Emperor Ôjin, Impress Jingū, and Hime-gami, which were first enshrined in the Usa Hachiman-gū of Ôita Prefecture and thence came to be enshrined in many Hachiman shrines throughout the entire country. Besides being worshipped as the deity of war, the deity Hachiman is the object of deep devotion by many classes.

Haiden: Oratory, the Hall of Worship. ⟶ Jinja shaden.

Hairei: In Shinto, the formal manner of paying worship to a deity. Advancing in front of the deity, one first bows deeply twice, then claps the hands twice, and then makes another deep bow. It is proper etiquette to offer a *tama-gushi** when performing *Hairei.*

Hakama.

Hakama : Part of formal costume of Shinto priests. The *hakama* worn today by Shinto priests are of three colors: purple with insignia, purple, and light blue; these three types are worn according to rank.

Hakusan : Refers to the three deities Kukuri-hime-no-kami (the goddess who, in the age of the gods, arbitrated between the two deities Izanagi when they quarrelled at the hill Yomo-tsu-hira-saka), Izanagi, and Izanami, who are enshrined in the Shira-yama-hime Jinja in Ishikawa Prefecture, as well as in its branch shrines, the so-called Hakusan shrines, throughout the country. Devotion to the Shira-yama-hime Jinja originates in religious worship of the mountain is the most famous mountain in the Hokuriku region.

Hakushu : ⟶ Kashiwade.

Harae-do : A building provided in shrines to purify the body and minds of priests and participants before the performance of a religious ceremony. In some shrines there is no separate building, and a certain place is set aside for the purpose.

Harai : The purification ceremonies of Shinto. The removal of all sins, pollutions, and disasters by praying to the gods. The return to a condition in which one can approach the gods, by purifying body and mind. The correct ancient pronunciation is *harae,* but today the word is usually pronounced *harai.* According to mythology, *harae* originated when the god Izanagi removed the pollutions he had received when he traveled to the land of *Yomi.** Besides being performed occasionally to remove sin, pollution, and disaster when the need arises, *harae* is always performed at religious ceremonies. In the case of religious ceremonies, *harae* always precedes the ceremonies. In antiquity two types of *harae,* called *yoshi-harae* and *ashi-harae* (literally, purification of good and purification of evil), were performed, but the meaning of these terms is not clear. *Ô-harae* was a national *harae* performed regularly twice a year and also occasionally as need arose. In Shinto, not only were the sins, pollutions, and disasters of the individual removed, but also evils and mishaps were removed from the whole nation and people, by which new life began, and the blessings of the gods were brought down. The *norito** used at the *Ô-harae* is called *Ô-barae-no-kotoba.* It was the duty of the Nakatomi clan to pronounce it, and therefore it is also called by the name *Nakatomi no harae.* *Ô-harae* is today performed, centered around the shrines, on the last days of June and December of each year. *Harae* being one of the most important ceremonies in Shinto, various forms of *harae* developed, such as *nagoshi no harae,* and *mi no hi no harae.* There is also a general practice of reciting alone or in unison, with slight change, the *Ô-barae-no-kotoba,* which is regarded as a sacred scripture. *Shubatsu* is a *harae* ceremony perfarmed by priests before a ceremony or religious rite; the ceremony of *te-mizu* (purification of hands and mouth; see the article on *Misogi*) is performed, the *norito* of *harae* is pronounced in the place where *harae* is performed, and a wand called *harai-gushi* is waved.

Harai-gushi.

Harai-gushi : One of the implements used in *harae.* It is a wooden stick to which linen cloths or paper streamers have been attached; by waving it to the left, right, and left, pollution is purified. Other implements used in *harae* include the *ô-nusa,* a branch of the sacred tree or other evergreen to which linen cloths or paper streamers have been attached; and the *ko-nusa,* the small-scale implement used by each person to purify himself.

Haru-matsuri : A festival celebrated in spring. Together with autumn, spring is frequently chosen as the season for religious festivals. This is because in Japan, where life depends on agriculture, it is considered to be a matter of greatest importance to pray to the gods for an abundant harvest. This is also the reason why the *Toshi-goi no matsuri,* the festival for praying a good harvest, is performed.

Hassoku-an : ——> Saikigu.

Hatsuho : First fruits. At the occasion of thanksgiving to the deities for the autumn rice harvest, the best of the first rice shoots are removed and presented. *Hatsu-ho* means the first ripened rice shoots, or the first rice shoots to be offered. Thence, anything offered to a deity is called *hatsu-ho.*

Hatsu-miya-mairi : The first visit paid by a newborn child to the tutelary deity. Generally paid on the 32nd day after the birth of a boy, and the 33rd day after the birth of a girl. The mother or a close woman relative takes the child. It is a ceremony recognizing the fact that the baby has become one of the parishioners, and is the first of the ceremonies of initiation.

Hatsu-môde : "First visit"; the making of a visit to a shrine at the first of the year to pray for happiness and divine protection during the new year. Believed to be a very old custom, but that the medieval practice of *ehô-mairi,* or visiting a shrine standing in an auspicious direction, has influenced the practice.

Heiden : Hall of Offerings. ⟶ Jinja shaden.

Hi-machi : A popular religious custom by which a company of believers assemble at each other's houses on set days, such as the 15th of the first, fifth, and ninth months of the old calendar, hold a religious ceremony, then spend the night talking, and worship the rising sun. *Hi-machi,* meaning "waiting for the sun," refers to the waiting for the sun to rise.

Hi-matsuri : A festival centering around fire. Usually, like the *dondo-yaki* of "Little New Year's" (*Ko-shôgatsu*) or the *o-hi-taki* ("fire-burning") of the mid-winter festival (*tôji*), are intended to pray for the restoration of the power of the sun. Also, such as the *hi-matsuri* of Yoshida-machi at the foot of Mt. Fuji or the *Shô-rei-sai* festival of Dewa Jinja of Yamagata Prefecture, there are some which possess the significance of divining whether the year will be a good one or one of ill fortune. At any rate, fire is considered to be sacred, to have power to destroy evil, is used as a sign of descent of a god, and is indispensible in illuminating religious ceremonies; its significance in religious ceremonies is great.

Himorogi : A type of *mi-tama-shiro,** believed to be the primitive form of the shrine. A piece of unpolluted land is chosen, and a sacred seat is erected there surrounding by evergreens. Today it has been abbreviated to an area of the purified floor, where straw mats are spread out and eight-legged tables are set up; in the center a branch of sacred tree is set up and *yû* and *shide* are strung on it.

Himorogi.

Hino-kami: God of fire. In Japan fire itself is not worshipped, but various gods are worshipped as the deities in charge of fire. Identified with the deity Ho-musubi-no-kami, but popularly fire-quelling deities such as *kôjin** are worshipped, largely with the hearth or stove in mind, and whenever there is a pollution, the ashes of the hearth or stove are changed.

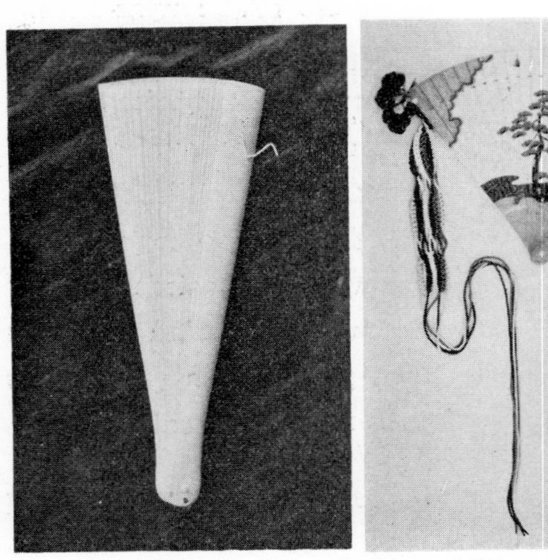
Hiôgi for Priest (Left), and Priestess.

Hiôgi: The fan held by nobles of the Heian period when formally dressed. Made by tying together with threads thin strips of *hinoki* (Japanese cypress) wood. The numbers of strips of wood differed according to the rank. Held today by Shinto priests when in formal costume. The *hiôgi* held by priestess, called *akome-ôgi,* is of extremely bright colors.

Hirata, Atsutane: Becoming a follower of Motoori Norinaga after the latter's death, he not only carried on Norinaga's leaning, but led this learning into actual practice and contributed to the revival of Shinto. Possessing a voluminous knowledge, he wrote not only about the Japanese classics, but also studied and criticised Buddhism, Confucianism and Christianity. He was the one among the scholars of the Fukko school Shinto who left behind him the most varied and richest writings.

Hito: Man. There are many who believe the theory that the etymology of the word *hito* is "place where a spirit is." In ancient vocabulary, human beings are called *ao-hito-gusa* (green-man-grass). This is a word of blessing comparing the human race to the green grass which grows up in a thriving manner. There is also the term *ame no masu-hito* (heavenly-increasing-man), which means "sacred human beings increasing infinity." In other words, man is a being living under the blessing of the gods and fated to prosper in happiness. Each man should feel happiness and duty at the thought that he has divine ancestors, is given a sacred soul, a sacred body, and a sacred mission, and lives as the co-operator in building the ideal world of the gods.

Hô: The outer garment worn above the garments called *sokutai, ikan,* and *saifuku.** In ancient days, the color of the *hô* was different for each scale of court rank, and the colors were purple, red, green, light blue, and yellow; but today the colors are black, red, and light blue.

Hô.

Hôbei: The presentation of *heihaku,* or offerings, to be used by a deity. *Heihaku* literally means cloth, but includes also clothing, paper, jewels, weapons, money, and utensils. In previous days because offerings were presented by the Imperial Court and the local government certain shrines were called *Kampeisha* (literally, shrine to which official offerings are presented from the Imperial Court) and *Kokuheisha* (literally, shrine to which offerings are presented from the local government). Today the custom is to present offering from the *Jinja Honchô.**

Hokora: Name of an extremely small shrine. Originally, *hokora* meant a storage building (*kura*) of beautiful form, and was used to refer to sacred storehouse and shrine buildings. Today, however, it is usually used to refer to small wayside shrines.

Hon-den: Inner Sanctuary, the Main Shrine. ⟶ Jinja shaden.

Hongu: Also called *honsha.** The central shrine in which dwells a particular deity. Used in distinction to *bekkû, oku-miya,* massha,** etc.

Honji suijaku setsu: Originally, a Buddhist term. A type, or theory of Shinto-Buddhist syncretism (see *Shinbutsu shûgô*). The Buddha as a metaphysical being is called *honji,* on the fundamental and original reality or source, and the Buddha as a historical being (Sakyamuni) is called *suijaku,* or the appearances or traces manifested. This theory was imported to Japan and used to explain the relation between Shinto gods and Buddhas; here the Buddhas were regarded as the *honji,* and the Shinto gods as their incarnations, or *suijaku.* Theoretically, *honji* and *suijaku* are an indivisible unity and there is no question of valuing one more highly than the other; but in the early Nara period the *honji* was regarded as more important than the *suijaku.* Gradually they both came to be regarded as one; and in the Kamakura period the Shintoists proposed the opposite theory, that the Shinto gods were the *honji* and the Buddhas the *suijaku*. This theory was called *han-honji suijaku setsu* (or *shimpon-butsujû setsu*).

Hon-sha : The shrine building dedicated to the principal deity of a shrine.

Ichi-no-miya : An old appelation for the representative shrine of a certain region. Its origin is not clear. Because of the growing laxity in principle after the middle Heian period, shrine worship by the Imperial House came to be limited to the Kinki, or Home Provinces region, and the system of 22 shrines (*nijû-nisha*) was established. In the localities also, the most distinguished shrine in the locality was made the *ichi-no-miya,* or "first shrine," and after it, the lesser shrines were made *ni-no-miya,* "second shrine," and *san-no-miya,* "third shrine" in order to facilitate the visits of the local *kokushi* or govenor. Naturally, this practice also extended to the level of the country and village, but it is not infrequent that there were changes in the ranks of the shrines.

Iku-tama, Taru-tama : ⟶ Tama.

Imi : The original meaning of the word *imi* is "avoidance." Since in Shinto pollution is a thing to be avoided, that which presents an impediment to religious ceremonies is called *imi*. Also the period of mourning is called *imi*. *Imi-kotoba** are in Shinto words which are avoided and replaced by other words; *imi-na* originally meant the name of a dead person which he used during his lifetime, but changed to mean "real name," and later to mean the name which was given to a person after his death.

Imi-kotoba : The practice of placing a taboo on certain words abhorred by the deity during the period of a religious ceremonial, and using substitute words for them. The practice of tabooing words is mentioned in the Engi-shiki, and there are similar taboos among people engaged in hunting, forestry, and fishing.

Inari : The protecting the rice cultivation as well as the five grains. In the Shinto classics is designated as Uka-no-mitama-no-kami. This god is enshrined in the Fushimi Inari Taisha and many other Inari shrines; prayers and thanksgivings concerned with agriculture are offered.

Irei-sai : ⟶ Tama.

Ise kô: An organization composed of persons who believe in the Grand Shrine of Ise. Generally has a village or hamlet as its unit, sponsors religious meetings several times a year within its area, or sends representatives from its membership to worship at the Grand Shrine of Ise.

Ise no jingû: The Grand Shrine of Ise, the *Kôtai Jingû* or *Naikû* and the *Toyo-uke Dai-jingû* or *Gekû,* are the largest and holiest shrines in Japan. In the *Naikû* is enshrined the Imperial Ancestress Ama-teras-ô-mikami, and in the *Gekû* the goddess Toyo-uke-ô-mikami. The *Naikû* was legendarily founded in the year 5 A.D. during the reign of Emperor Suinin; and the *Gekû* in 478 A.D. during the reign of Emperor Yûryaku. The symbol of the deity of the *Naikû* is one of the three sacred treasures, the *Yata* Mirror. The *shikinen sengû*, the custom of re-building the shrine every twenty years, was stipulated by Emperor Temmu (reigned 673–686 AD) and first carried out by Empress Jitô (reigned 686–689 AD); it has been performed 59 times until the present. Since Ama-terasu-ô-mikami was enshrined by the princess Toyo-suki-iri-hime-no-mikoto during the reign of Emperor Sûjin (traditionally reigned 97–30 BC) and moved to the divinely selected spot on the upper reaches of the Isuzu River by princess Yamato-hime-no-mikoto traditionally in the year 5 AD, the shrine has continued to incorporate under its jurisdiction many subsidiary shrines. The Grand Shrine is the spiritual center of all shrines in the country, and the rallying-point for the faith of the Japanese people. Not to speak of the reverence paid to it by the Imperial Family, there are many historical evidences of the widespread popular devotion to the shrine, such as the popularity of spontaneous mass pilgrimages (*o-kage mairi*), the widespread use of *taima** amulets on family altar, etc.

Ise Shintô: A school of Shinto thought established by priests of the Grand Shrine of Ise from medieval to recent times. In its early period it contained Buddhist elements, and in its later period Confucianist elements were added. It established a Japanese Shinto theology placing purity and honesty as the highest virtues and teaching that these virtues should be gained through a religious experience.

Iwasaka: A place where a deity is worshipped in the open: a spot of unpolluted land is chosen, and surrounded with stones. This word appears in the *Kojiki.**

Iwa-shimizu matsuri: A festival celebrated every year on September 15 at the Iwa-shimizu Hachiman-gû. Anciently it was called *Hôjô-e,* and on the day of the full moon around August 15 every year, living creatures such as birds and fish were released into the rivers and skies with Buddhist rituals. Today it still contains Buddhist elements.

Iwau : The original meaning is to perform *saikai** and serve a god; but today the meaning is to conduct ceremonies for the purpose of blessing oneself or others, or to pronounce words of blessing. *O-iwai* is the ceremonies connected with the act of "*iwau.*" *O-iwai* can be performed without divine worship as well as with it, but tacitly the protection of the gods is counted on.

Izanagi-no-mikoto : A deity in the seventh generation of deities in the age of the gods. Marrying the goddess Izanami-no-mikoto, he became with her the first wedded couple, bore the terrestrial regions (*Ô-ya-shima-guni*), the bore mountains, rivers, seas, plants, animals, and men, becoming the god of the earth and of all things in the earth. His wife Izanami died when she gave birth to the God of Fire, and became a goddess of the land of Yomi. Izanagi went to visit his dead wife in Yomi, but broke a taboo and was forced to part with her; having come in contact with pollution, he feared that disaster would result, and went and performed *misogi** in the sea and cast out his pollution. Thus he is regarded as the founder of the practice of *harae.** The most important three gods born by Izanagi-no-mikoto are Amaterasu-ô-mikami,* Susa-no-wo-no-mikoto,* and Tsuki-yomi-no-mikoto.

Jidai matsuri.

Izanami-no-mikoto : ⟶ Izanagi-no-mikoto.

Jichinsai : ⟶ Ji-matsuri.

Jidai matsuri : A festival celebrated each year on October 22 at Heian Jingû in Kyôto City. On this day a procession winds through the city with people dressed as historical characters in the costumes of each period of the over 1,000 years (from the Enryaku period in the 8th century until the Meiji period) that the capital was in Kyôto (the Heian capital). Before the eyes of the spector is unfolded a veritable scroll of brilliant sights.

Ji-gami: A deity worshipped, in regions west of the Kantô region, in a corner of the garden or on the borders of fields. It is said that worship is paid to the spirit of the person who first started the village or the particular field, also that worship is given to one's family ancestors; and there are places where it is said that after a person dies, 33 years later he becomes a *ji-gami*. There is also a belief identifying the *ji-gami* with the *ta-no-kami.**

Ji-gami.

Ji matsuri: A ritual performed before constructing a building to worship the deity of the locality and pray for safety during the construction.

Jingi: ⟶ Kami.

Jingi-in: A government office established in 1940 within the Ministry of the Interior (*Naimu-shô*) as an expansion of the Ministry's *Jinja-kyoku** in order to increase the prestige of Shinto worship and to promote Shinto education among the people. Until its abolition at the end of the war, it was the core of shrine administration and held the leading position in the Shinto world.

Jingi-kan: The ancient government office in charge of Shinto worship. The *Taihô-ryô,* the basic law of 701 AD, stipulated that the *Dajô-kan** be the highest government office, and that the Jingi-kan be on equal footing with it. The *Dajô-kan* was an imitation of the T'ang Chinese system, but the *Jingi-kan* was placed on an equal footing with it in accordance with uniquely Japanese views. The *Jingi-kan* was in charge of everything concerned with worship of the gods and the system connected therewith. In 1868, the first year of Meiji, the *Jingi-kan* was restored in accordance with the ideals of *saisei-itchi*;* but in August, 1871, it became the *Jingi-shô,* and later in March, 1872, the *Kyôbu-shô;* it finally ended as an entity quite far removed from the original plan.

Jingu Kogaku-kan : Located in Nakamura-chô, Ise City. Educational establishment. Established in 1882 by order of Prince Tomohiko, the *saishu** of the Grand Shrine of Ise, inside the Hayashizaki Library in order to give a Japanese education to the sons of the shrine priests. In 1903 it was transferred to the jurisdiction of the Ministry of the Interior, and became a government school administered by the Jingû Shichô; located at Kurada-yama in Uji Yamada City, it had three courses: main course, research course, and regular course. Until it was closed at the end of the war because of the separation of religion and the state, it continued to send forth many leaders in the Shinto and educational worlds. In 1952, students for the priesthood, and in 1955 two courses in Japanese studies were established under the Grand Shrine of Ise, thus the Jingû Kôgaku-kan made a second start, having as its objects the education of children of the shrine priests and the promotion of Shinto studies, and pursuing an educational program intended to unite practice and knowledge in the sacred shrine precincts.

Jingû taima : A kind of amulet distributed by the Grand Shrine of Ise. At present (1957) 6,800,000 of them are possessed by worshippers and enshrined on the *kami-dana* in their homes.

Jinja : Word meaning Shinto shrine, a building and place where is enshrined the the spirit of a deity or deities. There are about 80,000 in the entire country. When distributed among the over 3,800 cities and villages in the country (1956 census), there are on the average more than 20 shrines to one city or village; and when distributed among the old *ô-aza* villages of the Tokugawa era, there was one shrine to one village. It is obvious that the shrines were the matrix from which the villages developed. The shrines assume various forms, large and small, in accordance with their history; but all are located in pure natural surroundings of great beauty and contain *Honden,* or Main Shrine, or Inner Sanctuary, as well as *Haiden,* or Oratory, or Hall of Worship, *Norito-den,* or Hall of Reciting Prayers, *Heiden,* or Hall of Offerings, *Kagura-den,** or Stage for Ceremonial Dance, *Shamusho,** or Shrine Office, *torii,** and *te-mizu-ya,** or Hand-Washing Building. In all shrines *shinshoku,** or Shinto priests, officiate at religious ceremonies. The management of the shrines is carried on by committees chosen from among the priests and *uji-ko,** or parishioners, and by the *uji-ko sôdai,* or parishioner representatives; upkeep of the shrine is managed by the offerings of faith of the *uji-ko* and worshippers. Shrines were born and developed through the religious needs of their *uji-ko* and can be called religious symbols born out of the necessities of the Japanese people in their social life, which centers on bonds of kinship and local ties.

Jinja-chô : Branch office of the Association of Shinto Shrines located in each urban or rural prefecture is called *Jinja-chô.*

Jinja Honchô : An organization of shrines of the entire nation, born by the common desire of all the shrines detached from state support by the GHQ order denationalizing Shinto in 1945. *Jinja Honchô* is the name of order as well as of religious association office. Today, 97 per cent of all the shrines in the country, a total of around 80,000 shrines, and 16,000 priests belong to it. Revering the Grand Shrine of Ise as its spiritual head, it is working for the prosperity of Shrine Shinto and the elevation of right principles. Its head office is in Tôkyô, and branches (*Jinja-chô*)* are located throughout the country.

Jinja kyoku : The government bureau under the Ministry of the Interior (*Naimu-shô*) which, until 1940, deal with administration of shrines and the Shinto priesthood. In 1877, with the abolition of the *Kyôbu-shô,* these matters were transferred to the *Shaji-kyoku,* a bureau of the Ministry of the Interior dealing with Shinto and Buddhist affairs simultaneously; then again, in April, 1900, the *Shaji-kyoku* was abolished and split into two bureaus, one, the *Jinja-kyoku* dealing with Shinto shrines, and one with other religions. Later, with the re-organization of the Ministry of the Interior, the *Jinja-kyoku* was made the highest ranking of the five bureaus in the Ministry. It was divided into sections of General Business, Research, and Leadership, and made great contributions to the spread of correct Shinto thought.

Jinja saishiki : Regulations concerning the order and conduct of rites in Shinto shrines. Before the Meiji period different ritual forms were observed according to differences in shrines and schools of thought, but in 1875, ritual observances of all shrines in the country were made uniform. The ritual observances conducted today are those fixed in 1948 by the *Jinja Honchô.**

Jinja shaden : The shrine is composed of three types of buildings: (A), the *Honden,* where the spirit of the deity is enshrined; (B), the *Heiden,* or *Norito-den,* where religious rites are performed; and (C), the *Haiden,* where the faithful worship and offer prayers. The *Honden* is sometimes called *Shinden,* or Sanctuary; and in the Grand Shrine of Ise, the *Honden* is called *Shôden. Heiden* means literally a place where

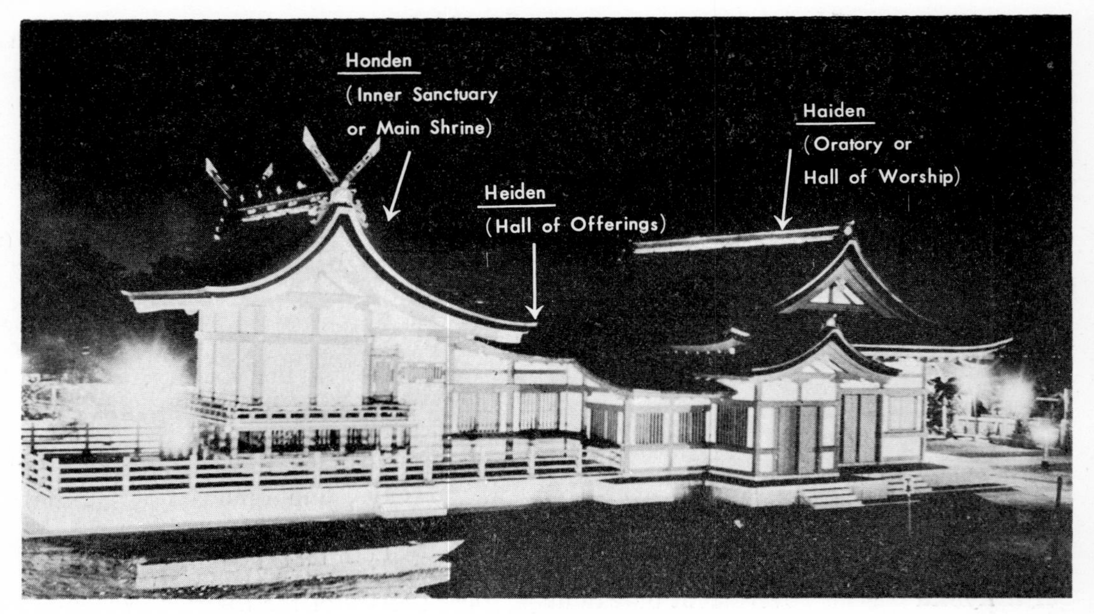

Jinja shaden (Shrine buildings).

offerings are presented. *Norito-den* means a place where *norito** or liturgies are intoned. The various shrines of today are all constructed in different styles, according to their various histories, but it is safe to regard them as being in general variations on this fundamental style. Before the fundamental style had been fixed, it is thought that shrines consisted solely of a *Shinden.* This is supported not only by the many examples of small shrines in the country today, but also by the fact that in the Grand Shrine of Ise, the spiritual head of all shrines, there are no buildings corresponding to the *Heiden* and *Haiden*, but the *Shôden* stands in the center of many layers of enclosing walls.

Jinja Shintô : The traditional religious practices which have been carried on around the shrines as Japan's native religion possessing a history of over 2,000 years, as well as the life attitudes which support these practices. At the core of this religion there exists a reverent religious experience which has grown up from antiquity among the Japanese and which causes them to experience the will and activity of the gods through various events of everyday life. Shrine Shinto possesses no founder of foundress, but through the interpretation of classical mythology and the re-evaluation of folk ways, it is gradually organizing its own theology. The politico-theoretical side of Shrine Shinto is called *Kokka Shintô,** or State Shinto. At present there

Jôe.

are in Japan some 80,000 shrines, most of which are under the jurisdiction of the *Jinja Honchô** in Tôkyô.

Jôe: A garment worn in religious ceremonies. Worn from ancient times by Shinto priests, but also worn on occasion by laymen when visiting a shrine to worship or during religious ceremonies. Consists of white silk or cloth tailored in the same way as the garment called *kariginu.**

Jôtôsai: A ritual performed during construction of a building in which the carpenters worship gods connected with architecture and pray for a safe completion of the work. The ritual is performed when the ridge-poles are made and are raised to their places on the roof.

Junpai: A pilgrimage following a definite course visiting definite shrines and sacred places. Became common in the middle Heian period. Some of the famous pilgrimage places are the 88 sacred places of Shikoku (*henro*), and the 33 places in Edo and Kyôto. The point is to gain merit by traveling around and praying through hardships and austerities; also widespread among Buddhist believers.

Jôtôsai.

Kada no Azuma-maro (1669–1736): *Fukko* school Shinto* scholar who, around the middle of the Edo period, first proposed *Kokugaku.* Studying the *Kojiki,** *Nihon Shoki** and other classics, he extolled the Japanese Shinto spirit of antiquity, free from Buddhist and Confucian influences. Together with Kamo Mabuchi, Motoori Norinaga, and

Hirata Atsutane, is numbered as one of the four great *Kokugakusha*. Among his writings there is *Sô Wagakkô Kei.*

Kagura (Ceremonial dance).

Kagura: A performance of classical, religious, and ceremonial music and dancing in Shinto. Origin is attributed to the performance of the heavenly gods on the occasion of Amaterasu-ô-mikami's seclusion in the cave, by which they succeeded in causing her to reappear; performed in order to pacify, console, and give pleasure to a deity. The *Kagura* handed down in the Imperial Court has an extremely ancient tradition; the words and music are of great classical value; and the ceremony is performed solemnly all night long. In the shrines, young *miko** (priestess) dance. There is also a popular *Kagura* called *Sato-kagura*, handed down among the people, which is performed on behalf of a deity. *Sato-kagura* also gave rise to professional artists. Today there are also performances of dance dramas of 35 scenes dramatizing myths.

Kagura-den: Building in which Kagura is performed before the deity. In ancient days Kagura was performed in the open plaza before the shrine, but together with the development of Japanese medieval theatrical arts such as the Nô and Kabuki the same type of stage came to built in the shrines as well.

Kaiga: Artistic representations of deities are made, not only in sculpture, but also in painting. Under Buddhist influence, *mandala*-type paintings appeared early, and there are many excellent examples still extant, such as the *Kasuga Mandala.* Portraits of the deity Tenjin (i. e., Sugawara Michizane) were made in large numbers as objects of worship. Religious paintings are of many types—including deities represented as men, as women, as children, as old men, and as Buddhist priests—and excellent examples are preserved in large numbers in the shrines.

Kai-i: Ranks of priests. There are four ranks, called *jô* (pureness), *mei* (brightness), *sei* (righteousness), and *choku* (uprightness). They are granted in accordance with regulations fixed by the Jinja Honchô.

Kaijin-matsuri: A festival in honor of the tutelary deity of fishing and seafaring. Among shrines enshrining *kaijin* (sea gods) there are Sumiyoshi Jinja, Munakata Jinja, Shiga no Umi Jinja, etc.; every year sumptuous festivals are celebrated there by seafarers and fishermen.

Kakuri-yo: "The hidden world." Whereas the actual world is called *utsushi-yo,* meaning the visible world, the open world; *kakuri-yo* means the hidden world, the invisible world. *Kakuri-yo* is the world of the gods, and is interpreted also as the world after death.

Kamado-gami: Gods of the hearth. Besides being gods of fire, they are also gods which protect the family and ensure the prosperity of the family. These deities possess a very complex nature, and are also viewed as gods of agricultural cultivation. The names assigned to them are Oki-tsu-hiko and Oki-tsu-hime, but in popular belief there are many regions where they are called *O-kama-sama* or *kôjin.**

Kami: Appletion for the objects of worship in Shinto. An honorific term extolling the sacred authority and sublime virtue of spiritual beings. There are numerous etymological theories, but none of them are acceptable. Motoori Norinaga interpreted the word as an appellation for all beings which possessed extraordinary and surpassing ability, and which were awesome and worthy of reverence; he pointed out that the word was used, not only for good beings, but also for evil beings. But he was unable to explain why evil spirits are also called *kami,* and he overlooked the fact that the term *kami* is also used for commonplace, weak beings as well. This seeming conflict should be explained by reference to the *koto-dama* belief in Shinto; this ancient belief had it that beautiful, good words bring about happiness and good, while coarse, evil words bring about unhappiness and evil. The deities in Shinto are infinitely numerous, and constantly increase in numbers. This fact is expressed in the laudatory term *yao-yorozu no kami* ("eight million gods."). These gods all make up a union, and are united in peace and unison. The beings which are called *kami* include everything from the spirits encharged with the creation and activizing of heaven and earth, the great ancestors of men, to all things in the universe, even plants, rocks, birds, beasts, and fish. These are divided into Heavenly Gods (*Ama-tsu-kami*) and Earthly Gods (*Kuni-tsu-kami*)—*Tenshin chigi* (the Heavenly Gods, that is, those whose home is in *Takama no Hara*;* and the Earthly Gods, whose home is the earth). In ancient times Heavenly Gods were considered to be noble and the Earthly Gods to be lowly; but today this distinction is not made.

Kami-dana : An altar (literally *tana,* shelf) provided for enshrining a deity in a part of the house of a Shinto believer. It is customary for amulets of Ise Jingû, the tuterary deity, or of the shrine usually worshipped, to be enshrined on this altar and for worship and offerings of food to be given morning and evening.

Kami-dana (Household altar)

Kami-mukae : The ceremony of summoning the presence of a deity or deities to a *himorogi** or temporary dwelling-place set up for special celebrations held outside of the main shrine buildings. The ceremony consists of the intonation of a verbal formula summoning the deity by the chief priest, the performing of the heraldings called *keihitsu,* and the playing of the *koto.* As a folk belief, *kami-mukae* is accompanied by various types of ceremonies.

Kamimusubi-no-mikoto : ⟶ Musubi.

Kami-okuri : The ceremony of sending off the deity or deities summoned to a special ceremonial place after the completion of the religious rites. The order of ceremonies is the same as that of *kami-mukae** and consists of reading a formula for sending off the deity by the chief priest, the heraldings of *keihitsu,* and playing the *koto.*

Kamo no Mabuchi (1697–1769) : One of the four great scholars of the *Fukko* school Shinto.* Receiving the teachings of Kada no Azuma-maro, devoted his life to the study of the classics, centering in ancient philology, especially that of the Manyôshû. His works, such as *Koku-i-kô, Norito-kô* are numerous, and he played a vital role in the revival of Shintô.

Kanda matsuri : A festival celebrated each year on May 15 at Kanda Jinja in Tôkyô. This festival was celebrated alternately every other year with the festival of Hie Jinja during the Edo period; there was a procession with portable shrines and with *yama-boko* floats. In order not to be beaten by any other festival, the Kanda-ites, who were the representative Edo-ites, put on an extremely brilliant festival.

Kanmuri : Headgear for Shintô priests. Used when they are in full dress of *ikan,** *saifuku**, etc.

Kanmuri.

Kan-nagara : An adverb modifying authoritative actions of a deity or deities, meaning "divinely, solemnly, sublimely, venerably," etc. The word *Kan-nagara-no-michi* (in accordance with *kami,* or in conformity with the gods' will) is a term used to designate Shrine Shinto as the orthodox Shinto and distinguish it from Shinto in general, because the word Shinto includes as well elements belonging to Sectarian Shinto and popular belief.

Kariginu.

Kan-nagara-no-michi : ⟶ Kan-nagara.

Kanname-sai : ⟶ Aki-matsuri.

Kannarau : An archaic word meaning: to conduct oneself exactly as determined by a deity or deities; to emulate the way in which a deity or deities acted. Contains the idea that man should not act wilfully and in defiance of the way of the gods.

Kannushi : At present, generally means *shinshoku,* Shinto priest. Anciently meant the head priest of a shrine or someone who, after strict abstinence, had obtained the qualifications for serving as a spirit medium for a deity.

Kariginu : A garment worn in religious ceremonies. During the Heian period it was the common costume of nobles and warriors, and originated as a hunting garment, whence its name meaning "hunting clothes." There are dozens of colors differing according to the age of the wearer and the season of the year.

Kashikomu : To take an attitude of respect or reverence towards a god or a noble. To respect the other with a spirit of fearful awe as someone towards whom sacrilege or disrespect must not be permitted. When *Norito** is pronounced to a deity, the verb *kashikomu* is prefixed to the verb *môsu* ("to speak respectfully"). *Kashikomu* means "awe," and is distinguished from "fear."

Kashiwade : One of the formal manners of paying worship in Shinto. Consists of raising the hands to the level of the breast and clapping them. There are numerous types, according to the way of clapping and the number of claps.

Kasuga : Refers to the deity enshrined in the Kasuga Taisha in Nara City. Was originally the *uji-gami** of the Fujiwara family, but later came to be the object of devotion of the common people, and branch shrines were established in various localities. The festival of this shrine is known as one of the three biggest festivals in Japan; the beauty of its shrine buildings and shrine grounds, as well as the flocks of tame deer, are extremely famous.

Kasuga matsuri : A festival celebrated on March 13 at the Kasuga Taisha in Nara City. It is said to have originated around 700 years ago, during the reign of the Emperor Montoku. Together with the *Aoi matsuri** and the festival of Iwa-shimizu, it is counted as one of the three *chokusai ;** considered as a typical example of an *uji-gami** festival, it preserves intact many ancient rituals.

Kasuga-zukuri : A style of shrine architecture. Represented by the *Honden** of the Kasuga Taisha of Nara. Like the *Nagare-zukuri,** is considered to be a style which arose after the Nara period.

Kegare : Usually means pollution. Thought originally to have meant an usual condition, and there are some who interpret it to mean the exhausting of vitality. In Shinto pollution is regarded as inauspicious, as the cause of unhappiness and evil, and as an impediment to religious ceremonies; pollution is removed by avoiding participation in religious matters and in social life for a certain period of time, and by performing ceremonies of exorcism or purification (*harae*). Until the middle ages, death of humans or domestic animals, giving birth, menstruation, eating meat, sickness, accupuncture, etc., were all regarded as pollutions; but today the meaning of pollution is gradually changing into a mental or spiritual sense. *Tsumi,* or sin, in antiquity had a broad meaning, and included pollution. See also *imi, kibuku.*

Keiba: Horse races. Horse racing is performed as a religious ceremony originally from the traditional practice of divining the god's will concerning the abundance of the harvest. The horse racing of the Kamo shrine is famous.

Keidai-chi: Shrine precincts. A definite piece of lands necessary for the shrine to erect its buildings, carry out its ceremonies, receive the worship of its believers, and preserve the beauty and dignity of its natural surroundings.

Kenpeishi: A messenger bearing offerings. At the time of an annual festival in a shrine, it is customary for *heihaku** offerings to be send from the Jinja Honchô; the messenger bringing them is called *kenpeishi.*

Kenzoku: Originally a word borrowed from Buddhism, meaning the various gods or messengers who are subordinate to an important deity. There are cases where they are worshipped separately as *mi-ko-gami** (child deities) in influential shrines; and there are also cases where they have been established in *sessha** and *massha** in small villages, where they absorbed the traditional village gods.

Kessai: ⟶ Saikai.

Ketsuen-shin: A deity worshipped by a group of persons sharing the same genealogy. This belief is close to the old form of *uji-gami** belief, but since in Japan there did not exist from antiquity any groups consisting entirely of purely blood relations, the *ketsuen-shin,* or "god of blood relations" can really be said to be the god worshipped by a group possessing subjective consciousness of being one kinship group. However. among these groups there are some kinship groups where clear traces are visible of a family splitting into main and subordinate houses; there are cases where such a group worships a family gods, but this is a recent form which has developed in recent ages.

Kibuku: Mouring. There is a custom of not going out for a certain period in mourning for the dead. This period and its ceremonies are called *kibuku, bukki,* or *buku.* The words *kibuku* and *bukki* are both made up of the same two Chinese characters, in different order, and are the Chinese way of saying *imi.** The word *buku* is also a word of Chinese origin; its first meaning is "clothes worn in mourning for the dead," and its second meaning is "mourning." Mourning is performed for a lord or relative; the length of the mourning period differs according to the closeness of the relation, and also differs according to the historical period. The many legal rulings prescribing official mourning are due, not only to the necessity for religious ceremonies, but because of the connection with absence from work due to mourning. Shintoistic practices and Chinese burial customs are combined.

Kigan: Prayer to the deity in which one believes. Prayers are offered at the household altar in one's home or when one visits a shrine, or prayer may be offered by repeating the name of the deity in any place. Also there is *gan-kake*, praying about some matter in which one especially desire divine aid.

Kô: A meeting for the purpose of spiritual guidance; a meeting for the purpose of performing religious ceremonies; an organization for holding such meetings. The organization is also called *kôsha*. There are both temporary and permanent types of *kô* and *kôsha*. There are also many *kô* and *kôsha* which, having religious things as their central purpose, also engage in activities such as travel, recreation, money-lending to their members, and mutual assistance.

Kôdô: ⟶ Kokka Shintô.

Kogo Shui: A work by Imbe Hironari, said to be of one or two volumes. Presented in 807 AD to Emperor Heizei. Contains commentaries on ancient words and practices, gives omissions from the Kojiki and Nihon Shoki, and presents the author's opinions about the Ise and Atsuta Jingû and about the position of his own clan in relation to the Nakatomi clan and the position of the Nakatomi clan in relation to other clans. Although it has the demerit of centering around the accounts handed down in the Imbe clan, there are many accounts worthy of attention.

Kojiki: A Japanese classic, compiled in 712 A. D. based on oral traditions. It relates myths, legends, and historical accounts, centering around the Imperial Court, from the age of the gods until the reign of Empress Suiko (until 628 A. D.). Shinto theology has developed largely through the interpretation of its mythology. The ceremonies, customs, taboos, magic practices, and divination practices of ancient Japan are revealed in much detail.

Kôjin: Commonly believed to be the god of the hearth, but there are also cases where *kôjin* possesses the nature of *ji-gami** or *yama-no-kami** and is enshrined out of doors. Also believed in some parts to be a demonic god or spirit of Japanese antiquity eager to seek vengeance; constant attempts were made during the middle ages to subdue *kôjin* with Taoist rites.

Kokka Shinto: State Shinto. The pre-war Japanese state distinguished the religious ceremonies of the Imperial Court and of the shrines from those of other religions; shrine rites and education were carried on as a public system, and the government interfered in shrine administration and policy. In MacArthur's GHQ order regarding Shinto, this system was called State Shinto and its abolition was ordered. So-called State Shinto is founded on the idea that the prosperity of the nation, the safety of the Imperial House, and the happiness of the people are blessings given when human politics coincide with the will of the gods; this train of thought was an honest spiritualism which treated preferentially the problem of the gods. This was called *saisei itchi,* or unity of religious rites and politics. In ancient Japanese the words for politics and for religious rites both were derived from the same root. There are some who regard the tradition by which the Emperor officially worships the Imperial Ancestress Ama-terasu-ô-mikami and the gods of heaven and earth as the fundamental condition of the Japanese form of government and who use the term *Kôdô* (Imperial Way) to designate the State Shinto system by which ideal politics is to be conducted in the spirit of *saisei itchi.* The term *Kôdô* was used with the intention of making State Shinto the only orthodox Shinto and of distinguishing it from Shinto in the broad sense; this term was especially liked by those who wished to harmonize Confucianism and Shinto.

Kokugakuin Daigaku: Kokugakuin University. Located in Wakagi-chô, Shibuya-ku, Tôkyô. In order to counter-balance the uncritical acceptance of modern Western thought at the beginning of the Meiji period, in 1882 an institution called the Kôten Kôkyû-sho (Research Institute for the Japanese Classics) was established, with Prince Arisugawa Takahito as its first President. Its principles were clearly expressed in its constitution, which said: "In the way of learning there is nothing more important than raising the foundation. Therefore, to clarify the national polity, thus making firm the foundation of the nation, cultivating the moral virtues, and thereby fulfilling the chief purpose of life, is an eternally unchanging law." In 1890, Kokugakuin University was also established to extend the educational activities: departments of literature, teachers' training, Shinto studies, and training for the Shinto priesthood were established; until the dissolution of the Kôten Kôkyû-sho in 1946, these two institutions, sent forth many leaders in the worlds of Shinto, education, and learning. With the dissolution of the Kôten Kôkyû-sho, Kokugakuin University carried on its educational work, operating a Graduate School offering Master's and Doctor's degrees in Shinto studies, Japanese literature, and Japanese history; the regular university courses offering majors in Shinto studies, literature, and political science and economics; a special course of training for the Shinto priesthood; a training school for kindergarten teachers; and attached high school, middle school, and kindergarten. This educational institution is developing its own unique way of education founded in Shintoism.

Koma-inu.

Koma-inu : Originally, a pair of sculptured animals placed in or near a shrine in the intention of having them protect the shrine. Imported from the Asian continent, and later they also assumed a decorative significance. They are made of wood, stone, or metal. Usually called *koma-inu,* but sometimes also called *shishi-koma-inu.*

Kôshin : In the Chinese calendar, every sixty years and every sixty days comes one with the sign *kanoe-saru ; kôshin* is the name of this day and of the deity worshipped on that day. The belief in this day originates in Taoism, but is widespread throughout Japan, and there are examples of its becoming confused with belief in the *tano-kami** and in the *dôsojin.** A peculiarity of this belief is that the believers stay up all night on the night of the festival.

Kôshitsu saishi : Religious ceremonies of the Imperial House. May also be called "*Kôshitsu Shintô,*" or Shinto of the Imperial House. The most important ceremonies of State Shinto, or of *saisei itchi.** The origin of the ceremonies of the Imperial House is ancient, leading back into the mythological age. The Imperial Ancestress Ama-terasu-ô-mikami* imparted the sacred mirror to her descendants, bidding them to treat it as the symbol of the everlasting throne, and caused them to descend from Heaven to this terrestrial domain, Japan. Consequently her descendants, inheriting the imperial throne from generation to generation, have conducted religious ceremonies with the most ancient tradition in honor of Ama-terasu-ô-mikami, the gods of heaven and earth, and the many generations of Imperial ancestors. The ceremonies of the Imperial House include those in which the Emperor himself serves as priest and those performed by a priest as a substitute. Furthermore, ancient, mystic ceremonies which can be known by no one besides the priests directly participating are preserved strictly. The Ise Jingû, which preserves the afore-mentioned sacred mirror given by Ama-terasu-ô-mikami, has an indivisible connection with the ceremonies of the Imperial House. The public ceremonies of the shrine also have been, in a certain sense, merely different forms of the same ceremonies of the Imperial House. The religious ceremonies of the Imperial House, since the GHQ order abolishing State Shinto, have not been treated as official state ceremonies.

Koto-dama : ⟶ Norito.

Kujô : Rank of *shinshoku** below a *gon-negi.* Exists in such shrines as Ise Jingû, Atsuta Jingû, etc.

Kumano : Refers to the deity enshrined in the three shrines of Hongû, Shingû, and Nachi, all located in the region of Kumano in Wakayama Prefecture. The Kumano belief was especially active during the middle ages; not only was there reverence from the Imperial Court; but because of the activities of the *oshi,** the common people also came to visit these shrines, and branches of the Kumano Shrines came to be established throughout the country.

Kumotsu : ⟶ Shinsen.

Knni no miyatsuko : The local ruling families which, anciently, swayed political power in their regions and which, even after they had become subservient to the Yamato Court, continued undisturbed in their lands. Gradually with the firm establishment of the central power, they gradually lost administrative power and finally came to hold only positions as heads of the religious observances in their regions. The hereditary priestly families such as the Senge and Kitajima families of Izumo Taisha, and the Aso family of the Aso Jinja, are modern remnants.

Kuni-toko-dachi-no-mikoto : Name meaning "Eternal Spirit of the Land." In the mythology of the Nihon Shoki, is the first deity to appear at the beginning of the creation of heaven and earth. Treated as a very important deity by, for example, Ise Shinto.

Kushimitama, Sakimitama : ⟶ Tama.

Kyôha Shinto: Sectarian Shinto. A group of religious movements which, while adhering to the mainstream of Japan's native religion, have started independent sects based on the religious experiences of individuals. Their establishment is relatively recent, all of them having began their activities in the 18th century. The main groups were divided into 13 sects after the Meiji Restoration. They can be divided into the following groupings according to the content of their religious faith: Pure Shinto Sects (Shintô Taikyô, Shinri-kyô, Izumo Ôyashiro-kyô), Confucian Sects (Shintô Shûsei-ha, Taisei-kyô), Mountain-workship Sects (Jikkô-kyô, Fusô-kyô, Mi-take-kyô), Purification Sects (Shinshû-kyô, Misogi-kyô), Faith-healing Sects (Kurozumi-kyô, Konkô-kyô, Tenri-kyô), etc. There is also a way of classifying them as: Sects centering around the spirit of ancient Shinto (Shintô Taikyô, Izumo Ôyashiro-kyô, Taisei-kyô), Sects which include elements of foreign religions added to ancient Shinto (Fusô-kyô, Jikkô-kyô, Mi-take-kyô, Shinrei-kyô, Shintô Shusei-ha), and Sects centering around founders or foundresses (Kurozumi-kyô, Shinri-kyô, Misogi-kyô, Konkô-kyô, Tenri-kyô). The Tokugawa Bakufu exerted itself in protecting already established religions, and as a result caused the formalization of religion. On the other hand, as the blessings of peace continued, from the middle Tokugawa period annual observances, popular religious fads, spontaneous mass pilgrimages to Ise Jingû, and regular pilgrimages visiting various famous shrines all became extremely popular. It was a period of luxuriant, over-ripe growth of religions; and since the objects of prayers were such worldly benefits as curing of sickness, protection from disasters, worldly riches, and success in life, the already established religions tended to become isolated from the religious demands of the common people, and the growth of new religions was accelerated. It was in these social conditions that sectarian Shinto grew up, and it was only natural that the founders as well as the believers of these movements should tend to consist largely of the common people. Consequently, although their doctrines can be classified as above, actually their content is not extremely well systematized. A large number of small splinter-sects, which had from 1877 to 1908 been forcibly incorporated into one of the 13 main sects, separated themselves at the end of the Pacific War and began independent activities.

Magatsuhi-no-kami: The gods who bring about all sin, pollution, and disaster, in other words, all evil. They belong to the land of Yomi, the Nether-world. *Maga* means confusion, complication, distortion. *Maga-goto* means "evil things." *Ô-magatsuhi-no-kami* means "Great Magatsuhi God." *Yaso-magatsuhi-no-kami* is the name of deities meaning "Countless Magatsuhi Gods."

Makoto : Generally used to mean honesty, truthfulness, conscientiousness. From of old Shinto has held that the gods should be served with *makoto,* that conformity to the will of the gods should be accomplished by *makoto.* Sokyô Ono asserts that the original meaning of *makoto* is "truth," and that *makoto* is the fundamental principle of Shinto common to all gods and all human beings. He also comments that it is not truth in the sense of an abstract, universal law, but that it is an individual, concrete value applicable to each separate case.

Manyôshû : Oldest Japanese anthology of verse, compiled in the eight century. Contains 4500 poems written from the fifth to the eighth century by persons of various ranks, from Emperor to peasants. Noted for its straightforward expression of grand, simple sentiments. Also presents valuable information about ancient religious beliefs, customs and mores, and thought.

Massha : Synonymous with *sessha,** or a subordinate shrine, yet the structure and the degree of reverence paid to *massha* are usually less than the *sessha.*

Massha (Subordinate shrine).

Mato-i : Target practice with bow and arrow, conducted as a ceremony within the precincts of a shrine at New Year's. Originally performed by marksmen choosen from the community as a means of divining whether the harvest would be abundant. There are also regions where an ideograph of demon is written on the target. In Chiba and Ibaragi Prefectures this observance is called *o-bisha.*

Matsuri : Ceremonies offering prayers, thanksgiving, or reports to, praising the virtues of, and presenting offerings to a deity or deities. Many Shinto *matsuri* traditionally hand down extremely ancient forms and spirit, and they are extremely rich in variations according to deity, shrine, and purpose of worship. There are also many cases where ancient ceremonies called *tokushu shinji* (special religious ceremonies) are preserved with great strictness. Generally the ceremonies of a *matsuri* are made up of solemn rituals, followed by celebrations of wild, frantic joy. *Matsuri* are named according to their kind or with proper names. The solemn rites center around presentation of *shinsen* or food offerings, recitation of *norito,** music, and worship, and are followed by a feast (*naorai*) at which the *sake* and food offered to the god are consumed. The joyous celebrations include a procession with the deity, dancing, theatrical performances, *sumô* westling contests, and great feasts. *Matsuri* is the most important thing in Shinto and many not be neglected. In the true sense, living prayerfully and obediently under the gods' protection is *matsuri;* life itself should be identical with *matsuri.* Today the formal ceremonial aspects are called *matsuri.* For example, the peasants begin cultivation in the early spring by praying for plentiful crops, and at the end of autumn they finish the agricultural cycle by offering thanksgiving for a plentiful harvest and present the harvest to the gods. During this period, connected with these basic observances, numerous *matsuri* are performed. The Chinese term for *matsuri* is *saishi.* Also, since it was thought that the Japanese people ought also, in its political life, to follow the will of the gods and lead a correct, peaceful life under the protection of the gods, it has often been thought that there is no government without *matsuri.* This is the reason why the tradition of *saisei itchi* has continued for such a long time; and the word *matsuri-goto,* meaning government, is a word synonymous and of the same etymology with the word *matsuri.* *Saigi* means the ceremonies of *matsuri;* and *saiten* refers to the entire *matsuri* including *saigi* and the joyous celebration.

Matsuri-goto : ⟶ Matsuri.

Megumi : The granting of a blessing. The bestowing of grace. *Mi-megumi* is the form used when referring respectfully to the *megumi* of a god, or a parent, or a person of high rank.

Mi : ⟶ Tama.

Mi-itsu : The lofty authority possessed by a deity. The dignity, majesty of a deity. *Shin-i,* or "divine dignity" is the Chinese equivalent for the word *mi-itsu.* The word *mi-itsu* is vulgarly pronounced *mi-izu.* *Mi-itsu* is sometimes used in the same sense as the word *shintoku.*

Miki : Wine offered to a deity. An especially important item in the food offerings. There are various kinds, according to the method of preparation. In ancient days was brewed especially in the *Saka-dono* (Wine hall) whenever a ceremony was held. After the completion of the religious ceremonies, the participants partake in this wine and thus share in the blessings of the deity: this feast in called *naorai.**

Miko : A supplementary priestess in shrines. They perform ceremonial dances (*miko-mai*) assist the priests at Shinto marriages, etc. Anciently, women who went into trances and conveyed the words of the gods were called *miko ;* today, independent of the shrines, this tradition still lives on among the common people.

Mi-ko-gami : Literally, " revered child god." The offspring of the principal deity worshipped in a shrine, to whom also religious worship is paid. For instance, in Yasaka Jinja, the deity Susa-no-o-no-mikoto is worshipped in the center as the principal deity, and to the west his eight effspring are worshipped as deities.

Mi-koshi (Portable shrine).

Mi-koshi : Usually translated as " portable shrine." Actually is a divine palanquin. An ancient vehicle used for a deity when traveling, visiting, or moving to a new shrine. When *mi-koshi* are used, they are accompanied by priests and large numbers of people in procession dressed in ancient costumes and carrying various articles in their hands. Also, the *uji-ko** (the believers of the shrine) in each area, or groups of children each bring out various *mi-koshi* for the same deity and carry them around in a frenzied state.

Mikoto : Has two meanings. (1) The words or command of a god or a noble; (2) a term of respect for a god or a noble. Today used only in religion to refer to the words or commands of a god or the spirit of a dead person, or to speak respectfully of such a god or spirit.

Mikuji : ⟶ Omikuji.

Mi-megumi : ⟶ Megumi.

Minkan shinkô : Folk beliefs. Shinto has combined with Buddhism, Confucianism, the Yin-yang philosophy, and other religions and philosophies imported in the past from abroad. This receptive nature has caused popular beliefs and popular legends to be accepted and absorbed into Shinto. For this reason there is a high rate of superstitious and vulgar beliefs mixed in with Shinto, but also, on the other hand, it is also of course true that these are at times replaced by elevated beliefs and refined into healthy elements. Since the scope of Shinto includes almost the entire Japanese people, there are rather wide areas in which it is difficult to distinguish living Shinto as it actually exists from popular beliefs. It is possible to say that quite a large amount of Shinto consists of religion transformed into a mass of popular beliefs. The fact that there are those who avoid the word Shinto and prefer the terms *Kôdô* or *Kan-nagara-no-michi** reveals the existence of a movement for purifying the faith by rejecting the vulgar aspects of Shinto tranformed into a mass of popular beliefs.

Misogi : A practice of removing sin and pollution from body and mind by use of water. Its origin is attributed to the god Izanagi, who purified himself by bathing in sea water. There is widely practiced a form of austerity in which *misogi* is combined with the Buddhist practice of *mizu-gori* (cold water ablutions); but in shrines it is called *kessai,* and the practices include taking a warm bath or splashing cold water over oneself, or washing oneself while standing by the seaside or by a river. Also, there is a ceremony called *te-mizu,* in which one washes mouth and hands. At the ceremony called *shubatsu,* salt water is sprinkled. In Japan, people who have been to a funeral sprinkle salt on themselves; water is sprinkled before the gate of the home morning and evening: and restaurants put little piles of salt at their entrances all these practices stem from *misogi.* The Japanese customs of washing and bathing are also related to *misogi.*

Misogi-harae : Both *misogi* and *harae* are observances to cast off impurities and mishaps and to purify body and mind. They originate in the legend of the god Izanagi, who purified himself from pollution at Tachibana no Odo in Tsukushi when he returned from the land of the dead, Yomo-tsu-kuni. *Harae* and *misogi* are often confused, but *misogi* is restricted to a purification performed by a river or sea.

Mitama-no-fuyu : Divine grace. Divine blessing. *Mi-tama* means the spirit of the god. The etymology of *fuyu* is unclear.

Mi-tama-shiro : ⟶ Shintai.

Mi-tama-shizume : ⟶ Tama.

Mitamaya : ⟶ Tamaya.

Mitarashi : The water provided for washing the hands and rinsing the mouth in order to purify body and mind before participating in a religious ceremony or worshipping at a shrine. When a natural river is used, the river is called Mitarashi-gawa or Harae-gawa.

Mito-gaku : A school of Shinto learning begun by Tokugawa Mitsukuni (1628–1700) in the Mito clan, one of the three Tokugawa houses (Owari, Kishû, and Mito). Its learning inculcates respect for the Imperial Court and for the Shinto deities. Its main writings are: *Shintô shûsei* (17 volumes), *Dai-Nihon Jingi-shi* (23 volumes), and *Jingi Shiryô* (17 volumes) by Kurita Kan (1835–1899). Besides these, there are collections and studies of the *Fudoki** and studies of the *Kogo Shûi.**

Miya-za : An organization by which a portion or all of the *uji-ko** of a certain shrine participate by turns in religious ceremonies of the *uji-gami,** also, the persons making up such an organization. Also called *tôya** or *tônin.**

Miya-za Ceremony for change of *tôya*.

Mizu-gaki : ⟶ Tama-gaki.

Mizu-gori : ⟶ Misogi.

Mono : ⟶ Tama.

Monoimi : ⟶ Saikai.

Motoori, Norinaga (1730–1801) : One of the four great scholars of the *Fukko* school Shinto. Around the middle of the Edo period, following in the footsteps of Kamo no Mabuchi, he finally perfected *Kokugaku* and became its highest exponent. His main work *Kojiki-den* not only became a guiding-star for the Shinto world, but also exerted a great influence on the knowledge and thought of later ages. His *Naobi no mi-tama* is a simple exposition of his theories.

Musubi : The spirit of birth and becoming. Also, birth, accomplishment, combination. The creating and harmonizing powers. The working of *musubi* is something most basic and significant in Shinto. This is because creative evolutionary development forms the basis of the Shinto world view. There are numerous deities having to do with *musubi,* such as Taka-mi-musubi-no-kami (Exalted *Musubi* Deity), Kami-musubi-no-kami (Sacred *Musubi* Deity), Ho-musubi-no-kami (Fire *Musubi* Deity), Waku-musubi (Young *Musubi*), Iku-musubi (Life *Musubi*), Taru-musubi (Plentiful *Musubi*). Taka-mi-musubi-no-kami is a *musubi* deity closely related to the gods of Heaven, while Kami-musubi-no-kami is one closely related to the gods of the earth; these two gods, together with Ame-no-mi-naka-nushi-no-kami, are the three gods of Creation about whom the *Kojiki** relates that they appeared at the beginning of the creation of heaven and earth and made the basis for the birth and growth of all things. Ame-no-mi-naka-nushi-no-kami is a name meaning "God Rulling the Center of Heaven;" there are many Shinto scholars who hold that all the gods of Shinto are merely manifestations of this one deity. At the time that Shinto was restored at the beginning of the Meiji period, there was a time when Ama-terasu-ô-mikami was added to these three deities, and these four gods were considered to be the highest gods. There are many groups in sectarian Shinto which preserve this view as their sect tradition.

Musubi-no-kami : ⟶ Musubi.

Nagare-zukuri : A style of shrine architecture. Represented by the *Honden** of the two Kamo shrines of Kyôto. This style, today the most widespread in shrine architecture, is considered to have been a new style born in the Nara period accompanying the introduction of Continental culture.

Naishôten : Priestesses who belong to the Board to Ceremonies in the Imperial Household (*Kunai-chô*) and who exclusively attend to religious ceremonies in the shrines in the Imperial Palace.

Nakatomi no Harai : Harai.

Naobi-no-kami : Name of deities who are the spirit restoring a normal state. The gods who remove all sin, pollution, and disaster, restores the normal state, and bring back the pure, bright, proper, and straight world of the gods. *Ô-naobi-no-kami* means "Great Naobi God," and *Kan-naobi-no-kami* means "Sacred Naobi God." See also *Magatsuhi no kami.*

Naorai : ⟶ Matsuri.

Natsu-matsuri : A festival celebrated in the summer. Since summer is the season when pestilences, as well as insect damage to crops, and unexpected disasters such as storms and floods, are most likely to occur, the summer festivals characteristically are intended to guard against these calamities. In this sense, the summer festivals of Yasaka Jinja, Kitano Jinja, and Iwa-shimizu Hachiman-gū are noteworthy.

Negi : ⟶ Shinshoku.

Nenchû gyôji : Traditional activities repeated each year by a family, a village, or the Japanese people as a whole. Includes such yearly observances as the New Year's celebration, the Girl's Day celebration of March 3, Boy's Day on May 5, the Moon-Viewing (*o-tsuki-mi*) of August 15 in the old calendar, the Bon festival, *Tanabata,* and the *Shichi-go-san** festival.

Nenchû gyôji. Carpenters' ceremony for the first use of the adze of the New Year.

Ne no kuni : Also called *Ne no kuni soko no kuni.* The subterranean world. The land at the bottom of the earth. Considered to be the same as *Yomi.**

Nihongi : ⟶ Nihon Shoki.

Nihon Shoki : A Japanese classics in Chinese compiled at the Court in 720 A. D.—at a time when intercourse with the Continent was beginning and national consciousness was on the ascent. Historical narratives covering the time from the age of the gods until the reign of Empress Jitô (until 702 A. D.) are contained in its 30 volumes. The first half contains many myths and legends, while the latter half relates historical facts; it was regarded from early times as the most reliable historical work. Together with the Kojiki, the parts of the Nihon Shoki dealing with the age of the gods are an important source for Shinto thought.

Niiname-sai : ⟶ Aki-matsuri.

Ningen-shin : Anthropomorphic deity. The *kami** worshipped in Shinto are exceedingly numerous, as is evidenced in the expression "eight million deities", and among them one of the conspicuous types is the anthropomorphic deity, a human being worshipped as a god. For example, Sugawara Michizane is worspipped as Tenjin; Tokugawa Ieyasu is revered as Tôshôgû; and the war dead are worshipped as gods in Yasukuni Jinja. The reason why human beings become deified can only be understood through the unique view of god and of man of Shinto. In Shinto, rather than man himself, it is his *mi-tama** which is revered and worshipped as a *kami.*

Ninjô-mai : Literally, "Dance of the *ninjô.*" *Ninjô* was the name of the conductor of the musicians performing *Kagura.* During the Heian period, the *konoe-toneri* (head of the Imperial body-guards) came to perform this function. Preforms as the master of ceremonies, a very important rôle in *Kagura.** Causing the *niwa-bi* fire to be burned, he ordered tuning and gathering. In present-day shrines, the dance of the *ninjô* has been preserved separately. It is a dance by a man holding in his hand a branch of sacred tree to which is attached a round rod.

Norito : Words addressed to a deity or deities. Broadly, the general term including *norito, yogoto,** and *iwaigoto.* Expressed in elegant ancient Jpapanese. The ancient Japanese believed that beautiful, correct words brought about good, and that words which were the opposite caused evil. This is called the belief in *koto-dama* (the spiritual power residing in words). *Norito* belong to this traditional belief. The style of expression is typified by the *Norito* recorded in the *Engi-shiki,** the law book compiled in the tenth century. The contain words of praise for the gods, lists of offerings, words identifying the persons originating and pronouncing the prayer, and the subject of the prayer, but they contain no didactic elements. During the period of State Shinto, the shrine *Norito* were those of the religious ceremonies conducted by the State, and the State determined the wording. At present, the chief priest pronounces the *Norito* on behalf of the faithful, and the contents and wording are not uniform.

Ô-barae no kotoba : The verval formula used in the Great Purification ceremony. Since in ancient times the Nakatomi clan alone read it, it is also called *Nakatomi-barae no kotoba.* It is contained in the Engi-shiki. Since its contents express well one aspect of Japaeese national faith, it has been respected highly as a Shinto classic since the middle ages. Consequently there are also many commentaries on it. See also *Harae.*

O-fuda : A tablet of amulet on which is written the name of a deity, distributed to faithful by a shrine. Made of wood or paper. Generally regarded as a symbol of the god, enshrined on the *kami-dana,** and reverenced morning and night to pray for divine aid.

Oha-guruma : A portable shrine used to contain the symbol of a deity when the location of a shrine is being moved. There are two kinds: the formal type with a roof, and the abbreviated type without a roof.

Oharae : A ceremony performed for the purpose of casting off the sins and impurities of the entire population. It is performed permanently on the last day of June and December, but may also be performed specially at times of pestilences or disasters or before the beginning of great festivals.

Oharai : ⟶ Harai.

O-hyaku-do : A definite action for the purpose of praying; the believer goes back and forth between a shrine and some definite place in the precinct for a hundred times, praying at the shrine each time. Practiced by individuals and groups. The object is to gain divine aid by repeating the same prayer countless times; often used to pray about sickness, disaster, or success. There are many varieties, such as *hyaku-do-mairi, sengori* (a thousand purifications), etc.

Okina mask.

Okina : Old man. In the world of legend, gods often appear in the form of venerable old man. This is true also of the world of music and drama. For example, it is well known that in the Nô play *Takasago* the god of Sumiyoshi appears in the form of an old man. The Nô play *Okina,* revered as sacred, is especially famous.

Oku-miya : A shrine which is, geographically speaking, located further in the interior (*oku*), i.e., is less accessible, than the *honsha.** As a rule, when there exist shrines at the foot of a mountain and on the summit of the same mountain which enshrine the identical deity, the one at the foot of the mountain is called the *honsha,* and that at the summit is called the *oku-miya.* The *oku-miya* at the summit of Mt. Fuji is in distinction to the *hongû* at the foot of the mountain, called Fuji-san Hongû Sengen Jinja.

Ô-kuni-nushi-no-kami: A god whose name means "Great Land Possessor." Also known by the names Ônamuchi, Ashihara-no-Shiko-o, Ya-chi-hoko, Ô-kuni-tama, and Utsushi-kunitama-no-kami. Said to be either the child or the grandchild in the sixth generation of Susa-no-o-no-mikoto.* Persecuted by his many brothers, he was repeatedly exposed to danger, but was always able to escape with his life because of the intervention of mysterious helpers. His kindness is shown in his saving a rabbit whose fur had been torn off by the crocodiles. Receiving the recognition of Susa-no-o, he married his daughter Suseri-bime and was designated as the possessor of the *utsushi-yo,* or actual world. There he punished evil spirits, exerted himself in developing the land, cured illness and imparted medicines, removed the disasters caused by birds and insects, and later presented the land when the grandson of Ama-terasu-ô-mikami,* Ninigi-no-Mikoto (the ancestor of the Emperors), descended from heaven. After this he was enshrined in the Izumo Taisha. Widely worshipped as a dispenser of happiness, this god also received special consideration from the State. Worshipped popularly as the god who makes happy marriages.

O-mairi: ⟶ Sankei.

O-mamori: A small tablet or amulet on which is written the name of a deity, distributed to the faithful by a shrine. Made of wood, paper, or metal. Regarded as a symbol of the god, it is constantly worn on the person in order to assure divine protection.

O-mi-kuji: Divination by lots; a method of divining good or ill fortune, of deciding the order of an undertaking, or of choosing a representative. Pieces of paper or sticks of wood with the various alternatives written on them are placed before the deity, prayers are pronounced over them, and then one of them is drawn. There are various methods of practising it.

O-neri: ⟶ Shinkô-shiki.

Oni: A spirit possessing a fearful countenance, great strength, and a near-human form. The mental image held by the Japanese of these monsters differs with each period. The ancient

Oni.

image was of one wearing a rush hat, a visitor from a far-away country. In the observances around New Year's, remnants of this belief are still recognizable. In general, however, spoken of as being a type of devil.

Ô-nie no matsuri : ⟶ Daijô-sai.

On-sashiha : A curtain used for concealing something sacred; in religious ceremonies it is used to cover the symbol of a deity or as an ornament in processions of a deity. There are two kinds: *murasaki no sashiha* (purple curtain), and *suge no sashiha* (curtain of sedge reeds).

On-sashiha.

O-shi : Considered an abbreviation for *o-kitô-shi* ("prayer-reciter") existed before the Meiji Restoration. Since the middle ages, *o-shi* were employed in Ise Jingû and the three Kumano shrines; a close relationship was kept up between them and those who asked for their prayers, the *danna.* The *o-shi* traveled around year by year visiting the *danna* in various localities and distributing amulet. When the *danna* paid a visit to the shrine, they would obtain lodging and quarters to purify themselves from their respective *o-shi.*

Oshiki : ⟶ Saikigu.

O-tabi-sho : A prescribed sacred spot where the portable shrine is temporarily lodged in the procession through the parish regions during the festival of a shrine. It is thought that originally the *o-tabi-sho* had an important significance and was the real ceremonial place, whereas the shrine was merely a storing place.

Otome-mai : Literally, "dance of a young maiden." Among the dances performed by women, the *Gosechi no mai,* or the five-movement dance, is the oldest. It originates legendarily with Emperor Temmu, who once was playing the *koto* in the palace of Yoshino, when an angel descended from heaven and danced, raising her sleeves five times. At the *Daijô-e* festival, five young women, daughters of noble families,—and at the *Toyo no akari no sechi-e* festival, four young women—were chosen to dance, holding *hi-ôgi** in their hands. In shrines there is also a dance of *miko** clad in red skirts called *chi-haya hi-bakama.* Today the newly composed dance *Ura-yasu no mai,* commemorating the 2,600th anniversary of the foundation of the Imperial House, is widely performed. Eight young women perform it; there is both a dance using fans and one using bells.

O-watari : ⟶ Shinkô-shiki.

Raijin : Literally, "thunder god." A divinity based on the phenomena of thunder and lightning. There are shrines in various localities in honor of such gods, and the deities enshrined are Kamo-wake-ikazuchi-no-kami and karai-jin. This deity was anciently believed to appear in the form of a serpent or of a child. Even today there are places where a ceremony called *raikô-sai* in honor of the thunder god is held whenever lightning strikes.

Reijin : *Gagaku** musicians. At Ise Jingû, Kasuga Taisha, Itsukushima Jinja, etc., there are *reijin;* they perform *Gagaku* and *Bugaku** on the occasion of religious ceremonies.

Reisai : The festival celebrated once (or twice) a year. It is the most important festival of the shrine; and a day having some affinity for the deity, or one connected with the foundation of the shrine is often chosen.

Ritsu : *Ritsu* is the ancient penal code. Infringements of the *ryô* (laws), *kyaku* (temporary laws), or *shiki* (detailed regulations based on the *ryô*) were punished in accordance with the *ritsu*. The *ritsu* (6 volumes) compiled together with the *Taihô-ryô* (701 AD; 11 volumes) is the oldest, but the oldest extant *ritsu* is the one in 10 volumes compiled in 718 AD.

Ryô : The ancient basic law comparable to the Constitution of today. Was the fundamental law from before the Nara period until the Meiji period. The oldest *ryô* was the *Ômi-ryô* (662 AD, 22 volumes) compiled during the reign of Emperor Tenchi; the next was the *Taihô-ryô* (701 AD, 11 volumes) compiled during the reign of Emperor Mombu; the next was the *Yôrô-ryô* (718 AD, 10 volumes), during the reign of Empress Genshô, which is still extant. The *Jingi-ryô* (Laws Concerning the Gods) contained therein are connected with Shinto and show the regulations concerning the ceremonies of the coronation of the Emperors as well as the main festivals celebrated every year.

Ryôbu Shintô : There are two meanings. First, refers broadly to the Shintô of Buddhist-Shinto syncretism. For example, the Shingon Shintô* of the Shingon sect, the Tendai Shintô* of the Tendai sect, and the Hokke Shintô of the Nichiren sect. Second, refers to Shingon Shintô, interpreted mainly in accordance with the doctrines of the Shingon sect.

Ryôbu Shûgô Shintô : ⟶ Shingon Shintô.

Saifuku.

Saifuku : A costume worn in religious ceremonies. Made of white silk, it is tailored in the same way as the costume called *ikan.* Today it is the formal costume of Shinto priests.

Saigi : ⟶ Matsuri

Saijitsu : The day on which a festival is performed. The festival days of shrines are all determined for various reasons, but many of them naturally come to coincide. For instance, the beginning of spring planting and the autumn harvest season make up special seasons, and these are the seasons for celebrating the *uji-gami** festival. Also, summer is considered the season for festivals to subdue pestilence and storm damage.

Saikai : The practice of a life of abstinence for a certain period of time before and after a ceremony by a person or persons serving in the religious rites. The person remains in seclusion in a building called *imi-ya,* bathes frequently, practices abstinence in food to purify body and soul, avoids contact with death and sickness, and concentrates his full mind on religious matters. According to the level of the abstinence practiced, *saikai* is divided into two thypes: *ara-imi,* or rough abstinence, and *ma-imi,* or true abstinence.

Saikan : Building for the priests to remain in seclusion and practice *kessai** to purify body and mind before officiating at religious ceremonies.

Saikigu : Utensils used in religious ceremonies. The *sambô* is a tray used to bear the *shinsen**, or food offerings, usually made of unpainted *hinoki* (Japanese cypress) wood; under the tray (*oshiki*) is a stand. The *hassoku-an,* or eight-feet table, in a table used to bear *heihaku,* or offerings, *shinsen, tamagushi**, etc. The *takatsuki* is a sacred utensil used to bear the *shinsen.* Anciently were made of clay, but later came usually to be made of lacquered wood. There are two shapes of *takatsuki: kaku-takatsuki,* which has corners, and the *maru-takatsuki,* which is round. The *oshiki* is a sacred utensil, a tray with a brim of thin wood around its four sides.

Used to bear dishes of food and wine cups; in religious ceremonies used to bear the *shinsen*.

Oshiki *San-bô*

Saimotsu : Offerings made to a deity at the time a visit is made to a shrine. Articles or money presented before a deity as a sign of reverence.

Sai-no-kami : ⟶ Dôsojin.

Saisei itchi : ⟶ Kokka Shintô.

Saisen : Money offered when one visits a shrine or Buddhist temple. The sum tends to be small, and the general custom is to cast the money into a box.

Hassoku-an

Maru-takatsuki

(*Saikigu.*)

Saishi : ⟶ Matsuri.

Saishu : Supreme Priestess. Refers to the person who in the Ise Jingû ranks above the *Dai-gûji** and devotes herself entirely to religious ceremonies. At present this post is filled by Princess Fusako Kitashirakawa, the daughter of the Emperor Meiji. The post originates in the former practice of having an unmarried Imperial princess, called *mi-tsue-shiro,* assume this post, which was then called *saigû.*

Saiten : Matsuri.

Sanbô : Saikigu.

Sanja Takusen : A material of moral education on which was written the names and oracles of the deities of three shrines (*sanja*), Ise Kôtai-jingû, Hachiman Dai-bosatsu, and Kasuga Dai-myôjin. A legend said that the first appearance of the *Sanja Takusen* was in the pond of the Tôdai-ji Temple at Nara during the Shôô era (1288–1292). Probably was formulated around the middle Ashikaga period in the 13th century. Consists of teachings concerning pureness of mind, honesty, and benevolence, and has contributed greatly to the spread of Shinto doctrines.

Sanjû-ban-shin : Literally, " thirty gods." Because of the influence of the teachings of the Tendai Sect of Buddhism, from the late Heian period arose the practice of chosing thirty of the most prominent native Japanese gods and assigning one as the tutelary deity of each of the 30 days of the month. These thirty deities are called the *" sanjû-ban-shin."*

Sankei : Regular or irregular visits to a shrine to pray. Visits are paid to one's own *uji-gami** as well as other shrines in which one believes. Also, those living elsewhere usually return for the festival of their *uji-gami.* Sometimes, when one cannot go personally, he requests someone else to worship vicariously.

Sanku : The practice of scattering such things as rice, *sake,* pieces of cotton cloth, money in order to offer them to a deity. It is one of the forms of making offerings to a deity and is often performed in celebrations in honor of local gods or household gods. It is usual to scatter the offerings in the four corners and center of the ceremonial place. It is also sometimes explained that purification is accomplished by the mystic power of rice and *sake.*

Sanno : Refers to the deity Ô-yama-gui-no-kami, enshrined in the Hie Jinja of Shiga Prefecture and in the Hie shrines throughout the country. The term Sannô originated among the Buddhist priests of the temple Enryaku-ji on Mt. Hiei, who worshipped the Hie Jinja as their tutelary deity; still today the principal shrine and its deity are popularly called Sannô.

Sannô Ichijitsu Shintô : ⟶ Tendai Shintô.

Sannô matsuri : A festival celebrated every year on June 14 and 15 at the Hie Jinja of Tôkyô. The name of the festival originates in the fact that the shrine was anciently called *Sannô Gongen.* In the Edo period, whereas the *Kanda matsuri** was the festival of the townsfolk, the festival was celebrated to please the *shôgun ;* thus it was called *goyô-sai* (" official festival ") and had much pomp and ceremony. The gorgeous beauty of the floats rivaled that of the *Kanda matsuri.*

Sansha matsuri : Literally, " festival of three shrines." A festival celebrated each year on May 17 and 18 at Asakusa Jinja in Tôkyô. Called *Sansha matsuri* because Asakusa Jinja used formerly to be called Sansha Dai-gongen Sha or Sansha Myôjin Sha. Since this shrine was the tutelary deity of Asakusa in the Edo period, the festival is extremely brilliant and is famous for its performance of old-style *Dengaku.*

Sanshu no shinki: Three sacred treasures transmitted together with the Imperial Throne. In the past, possession of the status of Emperor was proved by the transmission of these treasures. They consist of a mirror, a sword, and a jewel. The mirror, called the *Yata no Kagami,* is a keep-sake given by the Divine Ancestress Ama-terasu-ô-mikami to her grandson Ninigi no Mikoto. The actual mirror is preserved as the divine symbol of the Ise Jingû, while a replica is preserved as the divine symbol of the Kashiko-dokoro in the Imperial Palace; both are manifestations of the goddess Ama-terasu-ô-mikami. The sword, called *Kusa-nagi no Tsurugi,* is a manifestation of the deity enshrined in the Atsuta Jingû, and its replica is handed down in the Imperial Palace. The jewel, called *Yasaka-ni no Maga-tama,* has always been preserved in the Imperial palace. Both the above were also given by Ama-terasu-ô-mikami. Since the middle ages, there appeared scholars who explained that these three treasures were symbols of the three virtues of wisdom, benevolence, and bravery; this theory contributed to the development of Shinto morality.

Sato-miya: In cases where a shrine is located on a mountain top or some inconvenient place, a shrine, called *sato-miya,* is built near the village at the foot of the mountain to facilitate worship. The term *sato* means a village, and *miya* a shrine.

Seichi: "Sacred place" a holy area separated from common ground by religious tradition. There are various types, such as natural forests, mountains, and rocks, as well as artificially produced *iwa-saka** (stone circle) and some of them reveal the primitive form of Shinto shrines. For example, the Omiwa Jinja even now has the mountain itself as its *shintai,** or the symbol of the deity.

Seimei: Purity and cheerfulness of heart. Together with *shôjiki,* one of the most prized virtues in Shinto; the spiritual element of *harae**. A pure, cheerful spirit is called *akaku kiyoki kokoro.*

Sendai Kuji Hongi: A work originating in the late ninth century. Consists of ten volumes detailing the history of Japan from the age of the gods until that of Empress Suiko. Although many of the narratives duplicate those in the *Kojiki* and *Nihon Shoki**, there are not a few old legends not found in other books and which provide information about religious ceremonies and thought. At one time was believed to be a forgery, but in recent years has been re-evaluated.

Sendatsu: Originally a Buddhist term. Since the late Heian period, as the practice of visiting shrines such as Kumano and Yoshino became more and more popular, a person who would serve as a guide for the believers on their pilgrimages and who would explain religious matters came to be called a *sendatsu.*

Sengû: A ceremony in a shrine in which the deity is removed to a new shrine building. In ancient days, when shrines were simple buildings, it is thought that the shrine buildings were renewed every year and ceremonies were performed to gain the deity's blessing. Consequently, *sengû* does not consist merely in making a new shrine building, but its significance consists in the fact of expecting the deity's further blessings.

Sessha: Name of a subordinate shrine located within the precincts of a larger shrine. The deity of a *sessha* is subordinate to the principal deity enshrined in the main shrine.

Shagô: The term, such as *Dai-jingû, Jingû, Gû, Taisha, Jinja, Sha*, attached to a shrine. There are also some exceptional cases in which a name of the deity enshrined is used as is for a *shagô.* The title of *Jingû* is the highest appellation, applied to the two shrines of Ise; the other shrines to which the title *Jingû* is applied are either special shrines enshrined Imperial ancestors or Emperors, or else shrines of especially distinguished background. The term *Gû* is also applied only to shrines enshrining an Emperor or a member of the Imperial family, or else to a shrine with some especially important historical background. Tne terms *Jingû* or *Gû* were not permitted to be used indiscriminately. The term *Taisha* was applied to shrines, such as the Izumo Taisha, which occupied a position of prominence in their regions. Generally, shrines are called *Jinja** or *Sha;* and the term *Gû* found applying to *minsha,* an ordinary shrine neither a governmental nor a national shrine, is a remnant of the customs of applying *shagô* to shrines which were overlooked in investigations. The above-mentioned distinctions were strictly held to from the Meiji period until the end of the war. Even today, which might be thought to be a period of no regulation, the use of the terms *Jingû* and *Gû* is not readily permitted.

Shakaku seido: The system of ranks of shrines which, until the end of the war, received government support. Differences of importance and therefore of treatment came about naturally as the result of the circumstances of foundation, the importance of the location, the degree of reverence with which the shrine was worshipped, and so on. Based on the distrinction in the *Engi-shiki** between *kampei-sha* (governmental shrines) and *kokuhei-sha* (national shrines), the modern system added two ranks—small (*shô*) and great (*dai*)—to each group, and made distinctions in treatment on the occasion of the presentation of offerings at the various festivals. Because of the lax principles which prevailed since the middle Heian period, there arose another system of subsidiary ranks including those of the 22 shrines in the metropolitan area (*nijû-nisha*) and the *ichi-no-miya** (the first shrine) and *sôsha** (the central shrine) in the localities. In May, 1871, shrines were classified into *kansha* (goverumental shrines) and *shôsha* (miscellaneous shrines), and *kansha* were further divided into three grades: *taisha* (great shrine), *chûsha* (medium shrine), and *shôsha* (small shrine), while *shosha* were divined into *fusha* (metropolitan shrines), *kensha* (prefectural shrines), *gôsha* (regional shrines), and *sonsha* (village shrines). Then in 1872 the system of *bekkaku kampeisha* (governmental shrines of special status) was established. The classification of shrines after the Meiji era into *kampeisha* and *kokuheisha* depended on the origin and status of the deity enshrined therein. With the end of the war, government support of the shrines was discontinued, and remains so until today. Therefore, now there is no official ranking system of shrines.

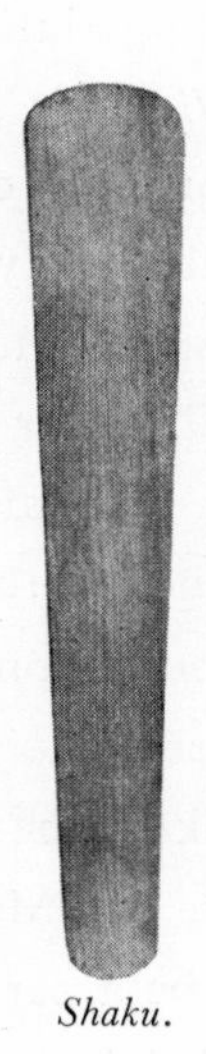
Shaku.

Shaku: A scepter-like article held in the hand by Court officials in ancient days when they dressed formally, held today by Shinto priests largely for the dignified effect.

Shamusho: A building provided with the necessary facilities for the priests to carry out the shrine business. At Ise Jingû this building is called by the special name *Jingû-shichô,* and at Atsuta Jingû by the special name *Gûchô.*

Shichi-go-san: An initiation ceremony. On November 15, boys who are five years old and girls who are three and seven years old, visit the *uji-gami**, or tutelary shrine, this custom is practiced widely around the Kantô area. November 15 was from ancient days the festival of the *uji-gami* in Japan; and it is a day when children pray to the *uji-gami* for protection at each step in their growing up and when they receive social approval.

Shikinai-sha: Literally, "Shrine within the *Engi-shiki.*" Refers to the shrines listed in the *Jimmyô-chô* of volumes 9 and 10 of the *Engi-shski**, which were entitled to state offerings at the times of their festivals. 3,132 shrines throughout the country were included in this number. There were two types, *kampei*—which received offerings from the *Jingikan**—and *kokuhei*—which received offerings from the *kokushi* or local governor, and these two types were further divided into greater or smaller.

Shichi-go-san festivalr.

Shikinen sengu : Removing the deity to a new shrine building once in a prescribed number of years. Oringinally, it is thought that the shrine buildings were renewed every year and ceremonies were performed to renew the power of the deity enshrined there; but permanent shrine buildings came to be erected, and the removal to a new building came to be carried out only once in a prescribed number of years. At the Ise Jingû, this removal is carried out once

Shiki-nen sengû.

in every twenty years; in 1953 the removal was made for the 59th time. Besides this, the Kasuga Taisha of Nara is rebuilt every 30 years; the Kamo Mi-oya Jinja of Kyôtô every 50 years; and the Nukisaki Jinja of Gumma Prefecture every 13 years.

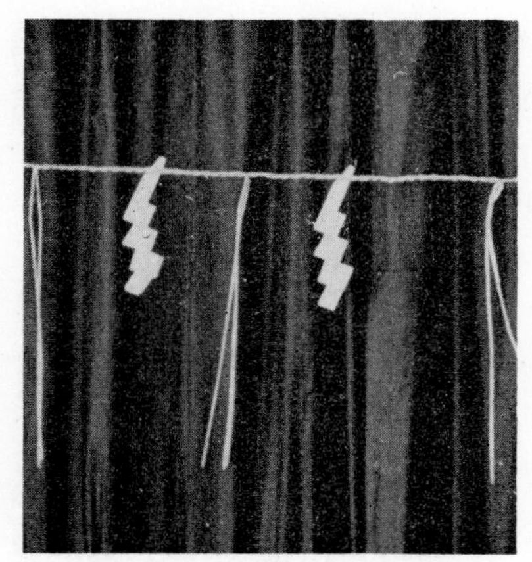
Shimenawa (Sacred rope).

Shimenawa: A sacred rope strung befor the presence of a god or around a sacred area in order to mark off the entrance to the area and to keep impurities of out of the boundary. Made by twisting new straw into a rope, to which is hung paper strips called *shide*.

Shinboku: A special tree or threes inside the shrine precincts. Sometimes *shimenawa** is strung around a tree which is regarded as sacred; and there are also many examples of worshipping a sacred tree as the symbol of deity in the absence of any shrine buildings. Believed originally to have been a tree to which the spirit of the deity descended.

Shinboku (Sacred tree).

Shinbutsu bunri: Separation of Shintô and Buddhism. At the Meiji Restoration (1868), the movement to restore the purity of everything Japanese took concrete shape in the Shinto world; as a result, on March 28, 1868, an order was issued by the *Dajôkan** which completely abolished the previous custom of syncretism of Shintô and Buddhism (see *shinbutsu shûgô*). It was forbidden for Shintô gods to be called *Bosatsu* (*Bodhisattva*), for Buddhist scriptures to be read before Shinto gods, for Buddhist priests to participate in Shinto worship, and for shrines to have Buddhist facilities within their precincts.

Shinbutsu shugo: A religious phenomena in which the two religions Shinto, the native religion, and Buddhism, the foreign religion, combined and co-existed. According to Buddhist doctrines, a person who has done good becomes a *deva* after he dies, lives in heaven, and encourages men in good and protects Buddhism. The word *deva* is often translated by the Japanese word *Ten,* but also sometimes by the word *kami*;* at the time of the introduction of Buddhism (in AD 552?), this word *deva* was interpreted in the sense of the Shinto *kami* in order to spread Buddhism among the masses who were deeply devoted to the Shinto religion. The syncretism of Shinto and Buddhism first began to appear conspicuously in history during the Nara period. When Emperor Shômu was about to construct a huge Buddha at the Tôdai-ji Temple in Nara (in 741 AD), he first commanded the priest Gyôki to report this to the Grand Shrine of Ise, and to offer there relics of the Buddha; furthermore, Buddhist scriptures were offered to the Usa Hachiman Shrine to beseech the aid of this god. At the completion of the statue (in 749 AD), a branch of the Usa Hachiman Shrine was built in the precincts in order to protect the Tôdai-ji Temple. Thus, the syncretic practices of building shrines in temples and temples (*jingû-ji*) or pagodas in shrines, and of reading Buddhist scriptures before Shinto deities and presenting scriptures to shrines, were all continued until the separation of Buddhism and Shinto in the early Meiji period. The embryoes of an explanation of this relationship are first seen in the early Heian period; this is the *Honji Suijaku* theory. From here, there followed the schools of Tendai Shintô, Shingon Shintô, etc., which are all Shintō theories explaining the syncretism of Buddhism and Shinto.

Shin-en : ⟶ Keidai-chi.

Shingaku : Today has become a term corresponding to the word "theology" in Christianity, but around a century ago was used simply to mean Shinto studies. Generally, it is only in the post-war period that the word *shingaku* has begun to be used in Shinto to mean "theology." The *kataribe* (narrators) of ancient Shinto resembled the bards who handed down the ancient Greek myths. The *Kojiki** was compiled from accounts handed down orally by a *kataribe* called Hieda-no-Are. The *Kojiki* and *Nihon Shoki** have been subjected to a certain amount of arrangement and selection by means of a comparative study of the old narratives, and in a certain sense are theological accomplishments; but theology with a real philosophical and apologetical background was pioneered by the *Honji Suijaku* theory, grounded in syncretism of Shinto and Buddhism. Under its influence there appeared Ise Shintô and Yoshida Shintô; various schools arose, and finally a new epoch began with the *Kokugaku* of Motoori, Hirata, and the others. Since the Meiji Restoration, the Shinto thought of Kawazura, Kawai, and Kakei have been noteworthy. In the post-war period, Ono, Nakanishi, Matsunaga, and others have made public new studies.

Shingaku : A religious and ethical spiritual movement preached by Ishida Baigan (1685–1746 AD). Based on Shinto (especial worship was paid to Amaterasu-ô-mikami and the *uji-gami**), it used Zen and neo-Confucianism to teach simply the ethics of everyday life to the common people; it spread throughout the country from its center in Kyôto, and even today is still alive. Since its teachings emphasized the moral training of the heart, the school was called *Shingaku* ("Heart-Learning"). However, this "heart" does not mean merely the same as the ordinary English word "heart." "Heart" meant for Ishida that which causes all actions and all uses of the human heart. There is a complete works of Ishida Baigan in two volumes, published in 1957.

Shingon Shintô : A Shinto theory relying for its interpretation on the doctrines of the Shingon sect of Buddhism. In esoteric Shingon Buddhism the unity of the metaphysical world with the phenomenal and natural world is explained by the two principles of the *Kongô-kai* (*vajra-dhâtu*) and *Taizô-kai* (*garbha-dhâtu*). In other words, the absolute is the relative, the phenomenon is the noumenon, and this principle is extended to explain that the gods are the Buddhas, for example that *Dainichi Nyorai* (*Mahâvairocana*) is Ama-terasu-ô-mikami. It is not true that this school of Shinto thought was founded by Kûkai (773–835 AD, founder of the Japanese Shingon sect); it seems to have originated in the late Heian to the Kamakura period. But, since an atmosphere favorable to syncretism of Shinto and Buddhism had been growing since the Nara period, it was not surprising that such a theory should gain currency. Kûkai himself was a strong believer in Shinto deities, and established the shrine Nibu-tsu-hime Jinja as the protecting deity of Kôyasan, the mountain monastery he founded.

Shinji nô.

Shin-i : ⟶ Mi-itsu.

Shin-i : ⟶ Shinkai.

Shinji nô : Nô plays performed as religious ceremonies. The Nô drama developed historically from the *za* (organizations of believers) connected with Kasuga and Hie shrines, and there are many local shrines where old forms of Nô drama are performed at festivals. In the Nô plays, there is one *genre* called *kami-mono* ("god plays"), performed the first in the program, in which usually a deity appears as the *shite,* or protagonist.

Shinkai: The grade or rank given by the Imperial Court to the deity enshrined in a shrine. This practice first appears in the work *Tôdai-ji Yôroku* (compiled around 1118), which records that in 746 the Hachiman Taisha was given the third rank in supplication for the cure of the illness of the Emperor. From the late Nara period, it gradually became customary to bestow grades and to gradually raise the grades of shrines on the occasion of prayers accompanying the moving of the capital, Imperial travels, coronations, wars, etc. At the beginning, fields proportionate to the grade were given in fief, but gradually, from economic and other reasons, the practice became one of bestowing merely formal ranks; and finally the whole system of *shinkai* was abolished after the Meiji period. In Japanese religious history, the study of *shinkai* provides valuable information about the comparative dignity of a shrine, the period at which it received fullest government support, and the ebb and flow of belief in it.

Shinkô-shiki (Procession).

Shinkô-shiki: A ceremony during a festival consisting of a procession centering around the spirit of the deity leaving the main shrine and passing around to various prescribed places. The processions are not all on land, but sometimes on sea. There are some processions, such as those of the *Gion-matsuri** of the Yasaka Jinja in Kyôto, which feature costumes of great historical significance and elegant beauty.

Shinmei: This word has two meanings: first, it is synonymous with the Shinto word *kami*;* second, it is another name of the goddess Ama-terasu-ô-mikami. Thus, the shrine dedicated to Ama-terasu-ô-mikami is called Shimmei-sha.

Shinmei-zukuri: A style of shrine architecture used in the *Honden.** One of the oldest styles, it is represented by the *Mi-shôden,* or Main Shrine, of the Grand Shrine of Ise.

Shinmei-zukuri.

Shinmon : A gate built on the avenue of approach to a shrine. There are various styles, such as *rômon, yatsu-ashi-mon, yotsu-ashi-mon, kara-mon, zuijin-mon,* etc.

Shinpô : Literally "sacred treasures." Treasures stored within the *honden** as articles used by the deity. Usually include such articles as sacred garments, cloth, canopies, mirrors, bells, pails, halberds, swords, bows, arrows, *koto,* and so forth.

Shinsen : General term for food offerings made to a deity. The offerings generally consist of rice, *sake* wine, rice cake, fish, fowl, meat, seaweed, vegetables, fruits or sweets, salt, and water; and are prepared in a spotless kitchen building called *Shinsen-den.* There are various kinds of *shinsen* according to the way in which the foor is prepared: *jukusen* is the name of cooked food; *seisen* is raw food; and *sosen* is vegetarian food containing no fish, fowl, or flesh.

Shinsen (Food offerings).

Shinsen-den : Rice fields consecrated for supplying the needs of shrine ceremonies. The main object is to harvest rice to be used for food offerings and also to supply funds for religious ceremonies. Supervised by someone designated specially (called *kami-yaku*), the fields are tilled without the use of horses or cattle, but are worked directly by men.

Shinsen Shôji-roku : A book giving the origins and histories of the various clans, compiled in 815 AD during the reign of Emperor Saga. In its 30 volumes it includes 1,182 clans, classified into three large categories: descendants of Emperors, descendants of gods, and immigrants (from Han, Paekche, Koryo, Silla, and Imna); these are then arranged in order of their dwelling places: Sakyô and Ukyô (the two main districts of the Heian capital), Yamashiro, Yamato, Settsu, Kawachi, and Izumi. The work is an important document in research in ancient Japanese genealogy and culture.

Shinshoku: Shinto priest; general appellation for persons who participate in shrine ceremonies and who carry on the various types of business necessary for them. In order to become a *shinshoku* it is necessary to have attended a school designated by the Jinja Honchô or to pass a qualifying examination. Generally, the highest grade is a *guji* (chief priest); in the big shrines there is under him a subordinate rank called *gon-gûji** (associate chief priest); then there are the grades of *negi** (priest, senior priest), *gon-negi** (junior-priest), etc.

Shintai: An object of worship in which the spirit of a deity is believed to reside. Or, a symbol or mediem of the spirit of a deity. The word *shintai* is of Chinese origin; in Japanese terms it is called *mi-tama-shiro. Go-shintai* is a polite way of saying the same thing. *Yori-shiro* is nearly synonymous, meaning, together with *mi-tama-shiro,* also a medium or symbol for the spirits of the dead.

Shintai-zan (Sacred mountain).

Shintai-zan: A special mountain worshipped as a sacred place where a deity or deities dwell. For instance, Kanasana Jinja in Saitama Prefecture, Suwa Jinja in Nagano Prefecture, and Ômiwa Jinja of Nara Prefecture have a mountain itself as their *shintai*;* in these cases, the mountain serves as a substitute for the *shinden,* or main shrine building. In Japan the belief is widerpread that ancestral spirits and gods of agriculture descend from particular mountains at festival time.

Shinten: Sacred books of Shinto. The historical schools of Shinto learning, sectarian Shinto, and other types of Shinto similar to these all have their own founders and scriptures comparable to the Buddhist scriptures or the Christian Bible; but the Shinto of the Imperial House, Shrine Shinto, and popular Shinto belief are not necessarily bound by the restrictions of any definite scriptures; they carry on their faith bound by the restrictions of the forms of their worship and their common ceremonies. Nevertheless, such works as the *Kojiki,** *Nihon Shoki,** *Kogo Shûi,** *Manyôshû,** *Fudoki** and other historical records are the source classics of Shinto, recording the Shinto beliefs of the ancient Japanese; besides these, the *Taihô-ryô, Engi-shiki,** and other legal compilations are valuable documents concerning the old systems and ceremonies of Shinto. Within these books there are contained mythological accounts and historical records concerning the origin of the world, the birth of the land, the appearance of the gods and of all things in the universe, the establishment of the nation and the relation of the gods to government, ceremonies of worship, manners and customs, Shinto attitudes and norms, etc. Shinto is not a religion which can be interpreted and understood solely by means of these classics; but neither can it be wholly understood without them. Consequently, the classics in general are viewed with importance among Shintoists, but there are many cases where the portions connected with Shinto in the *Kojiki, Nihon Shoki, Kogo Shûi,* and *Engi-shiki* are especially called *Shinten,* or "Sacred Books." There are also cases where others call a wider range of books by the word *Shinten.*

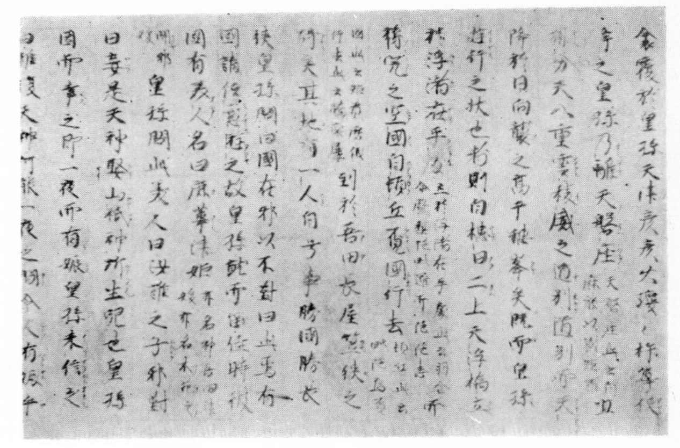

Shinten. An old manuscript of the Nihongi.

Shinto: A word derived from the Chinese term meaning "Way of the Gods," meaning "worship of the gods," "teaching of the gods," or "religion of the gods." Numerous deities were believed in among the ancient Japanese people; each clan worshipped its ancestors and common deities; and official life, inextricably bound up with worship of the gods, developed a political system of *saisei-itchi** (unity of religion and government). However, there was no name for this religion. A name to characterize this native religion first become necessary when Buddhism and Confucianism were imported from the Chinese continent; and it was at this time that the native religion was called *"Shintô."* Shintô was not a raligion depending on a founder, dogmas, or sacred scriptures, but one worshipping according to custom and time-honored system, revering ancestral tradition, and living and practicing by the guidance of the gods. Therefore, it had no sects. The Shinto which has preserved this ancient tradition in comparative purity is the Shinto of the Imperial House and of the shrines, while popular beliefs have developed with intrusions of other religions. Sectarian Shinto is a type of Shinto which has developed in recent ages by the activities of founders and foundresses, and in the post-war days so-called newly risen religions (Shinkô shûkyô), similar to Sectarian Shinto, have become independent in large numbers. Among the historical schools of Shinto there are Tendai Shintô*, Shingon Shintô*, Ise Shintô*, Yoshida Shintô*, Yoshikawa Shintô, Jugaku Shintô, Suiga Shintô*, Fukko Shintô*, etc.

Shintô go-bu-sho : Collective name for five books, the fundamental works presenting the main teachings of Ise Shinto. Thought to have been written in the latter half of the thirteenth century, which saw the establishment of the theories of Ise Shinto. The fundamental principle of the books is the elevation of the virtues of purity and honesty, which must be gained by religious practice.

Shintoku : "Divine virtue." Each god is endowed with unique powers of blessing and making valuable contribution; these powers are called *shintoku*. For example, Ô-kuni-nushi-no-mikoto is a god possessing extraordinary powers of blessing happy marriages. Sugawara Michizane (Tenjin) is characterized as the tutelary deity of letters. The special beliefs connected with certain shrines are connected with the nature of the *shintoku* of the deities enshrined there.

Shin-yo : ⟶ Mi-koshi.

Shinzen kekkon : Shinto wedding; wedding ceremonies according to Shinto forms, as one of the important ceremonies in passing through life, are widely distributed throughout the country. Originally weddings were performed in the home and were rites performed in accordance with folk beliefs, but since the Meiji restoration it has become gradually more and more common to use the shrine facilities. It is believed that marriage is realized through the protection of the gods and that children are born after receiving the spirit of the gods.

Shinzen kekkon (Wedding ceremonies).

Shinzô: A portrayal in sculpture or painting of a deity or deities the object of veneration, considered to be their *yori-shiro,* or dwelling-objects. Originally representations of deities were not made in Shinto, but developed by the influence of Buddhism. As sculpture, the wooden statues of male and female deities in the Matsuno-o Taisha at Kyôto are considered excellent examples of early Heian period Shinto art.

Shinzô (Image of *kami*).

Shiroki, kuroki: Literally, "white wine, black wine." Wine presented as *shinsen** on the occasion of the Nii-name-sai and Daijô-sai. According to the Engi-shiki, it was brewed from rice presented from regions determined by divination; the "black wine" was made by mixing ashes of the *kusaki,* or root of the plant called *yama-utsugi* (*Deutzia scabra*); and the "white wine" was brewed without this addition.

Shishi: Lion. No wild lion in Japan; its form was imported through China and Korea, and is often represented in the *koma-inu**. Also the *shishi-mai* ("lion dance"), performed wearing a wooden lion's-head, is often seen in shrine festivals, and at New Year's lion dance performers go from door to door to cast out all evils.

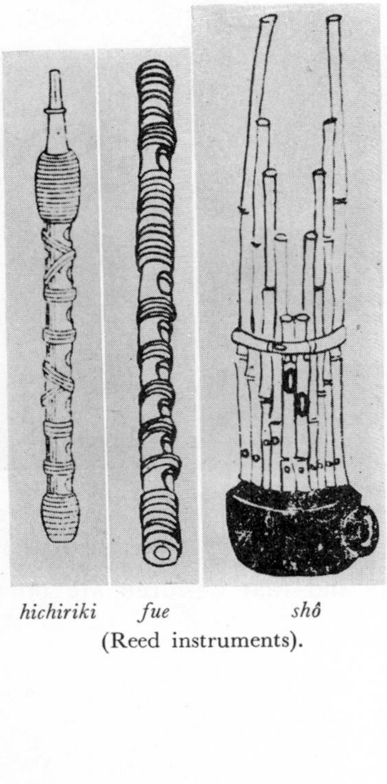

hichiriki *fue* *shô*
(Reed instruments).

Shô-gûji: The post which in ordinary shrines is called *gon-gûji** is, in the Ise Jingû, called *shô-gûji.* There is also a post called *shô-gûji* in the Fushimi Inari Taisha at Kyôto; however, although the pronunciation of the word "*shô*" is identical, there is a slight difference in the Chinese character.

Shô, hichiriki, fue: The reed instruments used in Gagaku are collectively called *sankan* (three reeds) and include the *fue, shô,* and *hichiriki.*

Shôjiki: Honesty. This virtue is one of the most highly prized in Shinto. It is said that the gods bestow blessings on the person who is honest.

The real meaning of the Japanese word is "correct and docile."

Shôjin: The observance of a life of abstinence for a certain period by those serving in religious rites or worshipping at a shrine in order to purify body and soul. Synonymous with the words *mono-imi, saikai**, *kessai,* etc.

Shôsai: ⟶ Taisai.

Shôten: Male priests who belong to the Shôten-shoku in the Imperial Household (*Kunai-chô*) and who exclusively attend to religious ceremonies in the shrines in the Imperial Palace. Divided into two ranks: *shôten* and *shôten-ho* (vice-priest).

Shôzoku: Originally, any ornamentation such as furnishings of a room, displays of objects. From the Heian period on, came to be a broad term for the dress of nobles and warriors. Today refers to the costume of Shinto priests in general.

Shubatsu: ⟶ Harai.

Soreisha: A shrine in which are enshrined the spirits of deceased ancestors; based on the Shinto belief that the spirits of the dead are to be worshipped as gods.

Sôsai: Funeral ceremonies. Shinto funeral ceremonies have been carried on because of the Shinto standpoint believing in the survival of the soul after death. However, mostly they are carried on in the home or in other facilities and are not carried on in shrines because of the intense abhorrence of the pollution accompanying death. During the Tokugawa period, because of the Bakufu's rigid prohibition of Christianity, the vast majority of the people were forced to have Buddhist funerals, and only a very few persons were able to have Shinto funerals. The present-day Shinto funeral ceremony is based on the teachings of Hirata Atsutane and embodies the ancient views of life and death of the Japanese people.

Sôsha: One of the appellations for the representative shrine of a certain region. Together with the laxation of principles in the middle Heiam period, Shinto worship also became loose, and there began the establishment of *sôsha* around the vicinity of the government office where the *kokushi* or local governor, dwelt; since the deities of the special shrines or, sometimes, of all the shrines in the administrative region, were enshrined here in this centrally located shrine, the governor was spared the discomfort of going around to worship at all the shrines individually.

Suiga Shinto: The word *Suiga,* taken from the writings of Ise Shintô, means the "descent of divine blessing." Suiga Shintô is one of the academic schools of Shinto. Founded by Yamazaki Ansai (1618–1682 AD), it is a Shinto theory to which the neo-Confucianism of Chu Hsi has been added, and which is a compendium of the various Shinto theories of the early Edo period. It regards the Nihon Shoki as the highest scripture, teaches unity of man and god, and makes the virtue of *tsutsushimi** the center of its teachings. Some of the characteristics of this school were the fact that the founder Ansai and many others were worshipped as gods while still alive, and the fact that, under Confucian influence, it preached Emperor-worship and an ardent patriotic spirit.

Suijin : Water god; worshipped at the source of irrigation waterways, lakes, ponds, springs, wells for drinking water, etc. From of old there has been a widespread custom of representing the *suijin* in the form of a serpent, eel, fish, or *kappa* (water-sprite). Another characteristic is that women played an important role in the worship of the *suijin.*

Suijin.

Sûkeisha : Literally "worshipper," a person beyond the geographical bounds of the *uji-ko** organization who nevertheless has formed a personal relationship of belief with a shrine irrespective of geographical considerations. The *sûkeisha kai* is a religious organization of these persons.

Sumô : Japanese wrestling contest performed on dirt arenas, in which the two contestants attempt to throw down the opponent or cast him out of the arena. Anciently, a *Sumô* contest was held in the Court in early autumn, in which contests of two teams of wrestlers from all regions of the country were used to divine whether the year's harvest would be plentiful. *Sumô* was also performed in shrine festivals to divine concerning the harvest.

Susa-no-o-no-mikoto : The younger brother of Ama-terasu-ô-mikami. A god possessing fierce might, he was guilty of disturbing the peace because he was unable to control his own power; after being expelled from *Takama no Hara**, he conquered a monster called *Yamata no Orochi* (Eight-headed Dragon) and saved its victim, a young maiden; thus he changed into a benevolent deity, performed many feats of saving others, and became a deity especially petitioned for salvation from disasters.

Suwa: Refers to the two deities Take-minakata-tomi-no-mikoto and Yasaka-tome-no-mikoto who are enshrined in the Suwa Taisha located on the shores of Lake Suwa in Nagano Prefecture, as well as in Suwa shrines throughout the country. Believed to originate in religious worship paid to Lake Suwa.

Ta-asobi.

Ta-asobi: A performance, carried out around the full moon of New Year's, in which the whole process of rice cultivation is carried out in pantomime from beginning to end in order to pray for a plentiful harvest. Certain shrines, such as the Akazuka Suwa Shrine in Tôkyô and the Mishima Taisha in Shizuoka Prefecture, are famous for this performance. There is also a summer festival called *ta-ue matsuri* (rice-field planting festival) in which rice is planted in a sacred paddy. Certain shrines, such as the Izô no Miya in Mie Prefecture, Katori Jingû in Chiba Prefecture, and Sumiyoshi Jinja in Ôsaka, are famous for this performance. In regions along the Chûgoku mountains such as Hiroshima and Shimane Prefectures, even ordinary paddy-planting each year is done to the accompaniment of drums. All of these observances are rooted in faith in the deity protecting the rice paddies.

Taisai: The most important festivals celebrated in all the shrines in the country are known as *taisai;* then, lesser festivals are called *chûsai,* and least important ones are called *shôsai.* At the *taisai* of Ise Jingû and other great shrines an Imperial Messenger (*chokushi* or *kempeishi*) is dispatched from the Imperial Court; and there are also differences in the offerings of food (*shinsen*).

Taisha-zukuri.

Taisha-zukuri : A style of architecture used in the *Honden**, the central shrine building. Taisha-zukuri, one of the oldest styles, is represented by the *Honden* of Izumo Taisha in Shimane Prefecture.

Takama no hara : Literally, "Plain of High Heaven." In Shinto, *ame* or Heaven is a lofty, sacred world, the home and dwelling place of the *Ama-tsu-kami* or Heavenly Gods. The word *Takama no Hara* is used eulogistically of it. Those who explain the myth of the descent of the gods from *Takama no Hara* as meaning a migration of peoples, seek to explain it as a geographical location somewhere on earth. No doubt this interpretation is mistaken. *Takama no Hara* is the Upper World in a religious sense. Also, there are some who interpret it as meaning a certain place in Japan in a religious sense, but this cannot be called the most common view. See *ame-tsuchi.*

Takamimusubi-no-mikoto : ⟶ Musubi.

Takatsuki : ⟶ Saikigu.

Takusen : Oracle; the possession by a deity of a human body, by which the deity pronounces has divine will with human words. As mediums, women and children were most frequent, but at times male priests also became mediums. A phenomenon often seen in the Shinto preceding the present observance.

Tama : There are two different meanings in this Japanese word: (1) A beautiful jewel. A mysterious, hard rock. *Tama-gaki* is the sacred fence around a shrine. *Iku-tama* is a magic jewel which increases life; *taru-tama* is a magic jewel which increases abundance. (2) Spirit, soul. Particularly a pure, lofty soul. *Tama-matsuri* is a festival to pray to, give thanks to, and satisfy the souls of the dead. *Ireisai* is a festival to console the spirits of the dead. *Chinkon,* or *tama-shizume,* or *mi-tama-shizume,* is a religious ceremony or pious practice to prevent the soul from leaving the body. *Ara-mi-tama* is a spirit empowered to rule with authority; *nigi-mi-tama* is a spirit empowered to lead to union and harmony; *kushi-mi-tama* is a spirit which causes mysterious transformations; and *saki-mi-tama* is a spirit which imparts blessings. These are called together *shikon,* or "four spirits." In ancient Japanese, beside the word *tama,* the words *mono* and *mi* also meant spirit. *Mono* and *mi* are low spirits, but there are many points which are not clear about the difference in their meanings and their mutual relationship. *Tama* is a divine or semi-divine spirit, such as the *mi-tama* of a god or of a person, the *mi-tama* of a land (the *kuni-tama*)—

the object of religious worship in Shinto is the *tama*. *Mono* seems to be the spirit of animals, and *mi* seems to be a concept viewing objects or bodies as spirits. At present, *mono* is used simply in the sense of being or object, and *mi* means body, fruit, or contents of a container. *Mi-tama* is the form of the word used to refer respectfully to *tama*.

Tamagushi.

Tama-gaki : The fence or wall surrounding the shrine buildings or around the outer borders of the shrine precincts. They are made of wood or stone, and sometimes are two or three—fold—each type has a distinctive name. In the case of the Ise Jingû, the fence is four-fold, and the innermost fence is called *mizu-gaki*.

Tamagushi : The type of offering presented by hand when formal worship is paid to a deity. Usually consists of a branch of sacred tree to which *yû* or *shide* (strips of paper) have been attached. They are also sometimes given out, like amulets, as objects to which the spirit of the deity is expected to attach itself.

Tama-matsuri : ⟶ Tama.

Tamaya : In Shinto, a memorial altar enshrining the spirits (*mi-tama*)* of one's ancestors. Usually, a mirror containing the ancestral spirits or a scroll bearing their names are put into a small shrine, which is placed in the "*mi-tamaya*" and worshipped on a slightly lower level than the *kami-dana**.

Tamaya.

Ta-no-kami : Literally, "god of the rice-fields." The deity protecting the rice crop; in ancient days was identified with the deities Uka-no-mitama or Toyouke-hime. Among the populace is among the most important deities, worshipped at different stages in the process of agricultural cultivation. It is believed that the deity descends from the mountains or from the heavens in the spring to become the god of the fields, and then returns again in the autumn.

Ta-no-kami.

Tanritsu-jinja : An incorporated Shinto shrine which is not affiliated with the Shrine Association (*Jinja Honchô*)* is callde *tanritsu-jinja*. The number of *tanritsu-jinja* is about, 1,000 in 1958.

Tatari : A warning given when a god is dissatisfied or angered at a man's words or conduct. When one meets with strange phenomena, mysterious destructive happenings, disasters, unhappiness, or sudden death, these are regarded as warnings given by a god.

Tayû : Originally, a respectful term for a person of court rank, but since the middle ages came to mean a Shinto priest; there are still regions today where Shinto priests are called "*tayû-san.*"

Te-mizu-ya : A building provided in shrines for the worshippers to purify their hands and mouths before worshipping.

Te-mizu-ya.

Tendai Shintô : Also called *Sannô Ichijitsu Shintô* or *Hie Shintô*. Said to have been founded by Saichô (767–822 AD), the founder of the Tendai sect of Buddhism, but is actually a type of Shinto based on the teachings of the Tendai sect which had its origin from the late Heian period to the early Kamakura period. It has its headquarters on Mt. Hiei (Shiga Prefecture). The god dwelling from of old on Mt. Hiei is called Sannô and is said to be a manifestation of Sakyamuni Buddha. It teaches that, just as Sakyamuni is the chief of all the Buddhas, so Sannô is identical with Ama-terasu-ô-mikami, the chief of all the gods; and the reason why Sannô appeared in Japan was to spread Buddhism in Japan, to pacify the nation, and to save the people in general. The Tôshôgû of Nikkô is a shrine belonging to the Tendai Shintô school.

Tenjin: Originally meant the "Heavenly Gods" but later came to refer exclusively to Sugawara Michizane (845–903). Michizane is worshipped as a revengeful deity or as the god of letters and is enshrined in many Tenman-gû shrines, beginning with the Dazaifu Tenman-gû of Fukuoka Prefecture.

Tenjin matsuri: The word "*Tenjin-matsuri*" refers in general to the festivals of the many Kitano Tenjin shrines located throughout the country, but usually it means especially the festival celebrated every year on July 25 in the Tenman-gû of Ôsaka. This festival, which features the procession through Ôsaka City on the Dôjima River of the sacred portable shrine on a decorated boat, is a typical example of a summer festival.

Tennô: As a result of syncretism of Buddhism and Shinto, the Shinto deity Susa-no-o-no-mikoto was called Tennô, but in the Meiji period this appellation was abolished. But the word is still generally used; the deity is worshipped as a god able to cast out and purify all evil and is enshrined in the Yasaka Jinja of Kyôto City, the Tsushima Jinja of Aichi Prefecture, and other shrines. The festival of the Tsushima Jinja, called *Tennô-sai,* is quite well known.

Tennô matsuri: The *Tennô* of the word *Tennô matsuri* is an abbreviation of *Gozu-tennô* (Susa-no-o-no-mikoto*). Anciently, during the summer a lively festival in honor of Susa-no-o-no-mikoto was held throughout the country to ensure freedom from pestilences and disasters. Today, the *Tsushima-matsuri* held every year on June 14 and 15 at Tsushima Jinja in Tsushima City, Aichi Prefecture, is also called *Tennô matsuri* and is quite famous.

Tenshin Chigi: ⟶ Kami.

Tôka: A Chinese custom brought to Japan by Chinese immigrants which became naturalized by combining it with the native custom of *utagaki.* Centering around the day of the full moon at New Year's, a procession for the purpose of stamping into submission the spirit of the Earth, as well as ceremonies intended to assure a plentiful year, were performed. In the Court it was celebrated on the tenth and sixteenth days of the New Year, but the former died out in the early Heian period. Today the *Tôka-sai* festival of Atsuta Jingû is well known.

Tokoyo: Japanese word meanding "eternal life," "far-away ideal land across the seas," "eternal darkness." The land of Tokoyo (*Tokoya no kuni*) is a world blessed with boundless wealth, pleasure, and peace; and those who come from there to visit this world were thought to impart blessings. Originally seemed to be a purely religious world, the dwelling place of the purified souls of the dead, but frequently actually existing foreign countries were also called *Tokoyo no kuni*.

Tokushu shinji: "Special ceremonies." Among the numerous ceremonies celebrated at a particular shrine, refers to those ceremonies with an origin unique to the shrine and possessing rich local color. For example, one can mention the *Mi-are matsuri* of Kamo Wake-Ikazuchi Jinja of Kyôto, the *Moro-tabune* ceremony of the Miho Jinja of Shimane Prefecture, etc.

Tô-nin: —> Miya-za.

Torii.

Torii: A distinctive feature erected at the entrance to the sacred area of a shrine, symbolizing the shrine, and separating the sacred precincts from the ordinary ground surrounding it. *Torii* are also erected here and there along the avenue of approach. There are many names according to the materials used and the shape of the *torii*.

Tori-mono: Articles held in the hand of the main performer in *Kagura** and other religious performances. In the *Kagura* songs there are songs relating to *sakaki* (sacred tree), *mitegura, tsue* (staff), *sasa* (bamboo-grass), *yumi* (bow), *tsurugi* (sword), *hoko* (halberd), *hisago* (gourd), and *kazura* (vine). It was thought that the spirit of the deity went into action through the mediumship of these nine articles; and the person who held these articles in his hand possessed the character of a medium for the spirit of the deity.

Tori-no-ichi.

Tori-no-ichi : Originally a festival celebrated on the days of the Bird (*tori no hi*) of November at Washi Jinja in Asakusa, Tôykô. Later came to be celebrated in various localities. The first day of the bird is called *ichi no tori,* the second *ni no tori ;* and there are some years when there is also a third, called *san no tori.* These days are flourishing *ennichi,** and in the shrine *engi-mono* (objects bringing good luck) such as *kuma-de* (garden rakes) and *o-tafuku* (a mask of moon-faced woman) are distributed. The *kuma-de* are especially prized among merchants in that they are believed to rake up happiness. *Tori no hi* is one of the 12 days in the old calendar named according to animals.

Tôrô : Lantern. Lanterns have been used in shrines from ancient times ; although there have been changes in the materials, use, and shape of the lanterns with time, the main types are stone lanterns, metal lanterns, and wooden lanterns. Also there are hanging lanterns.

Tôrô (Lantern).

Toshi-gami : A deity received into the house and worshipped at New Year's ; literally, "god of the year." There are examples of this belief in the classical scriptures. A special altar in the house is set aside for this deity, to whom abundant offerings are made of products of the sea, mountains, and fields and prayers are offered for abundant harvests during the year. There are regions where the deity is thought of as the god of food or the god of agriculture, or where the deity appears in the form of an old man and woman ; in Kagoshima Prefecture, there are places where on New Year's eve the young men disguise themselves as white-bearded old men and go around to visit the houses where there are young children, to whom they give rice cake.

Toshi-goi no matsuri : ⟶ Haru-matsuri.

Tôya : ⟶ Miya-za.

Toyo-ashi-hara no mizu-ho no kuni : Another name for the land of Japan; interpreted as being a laudatory term meaning "Land where Abundant Rice Shoots Ripen Beautifully." The terrestrial regions, when viewed from *Takama no Hara ;** are a world of imperfection. But there are not a world lacking salvation. Light is promised by the protection and blessings of the gods. The Shinto belief in *kotodama* consists in assigning a name of beautiful words, trusting in the blessing of the gods.

Tsuka : Sacred mound. A hill-shaped pile of sand or rocks used for ritual purposes; a good examples of worship of sacred places.

Tsuki-machi : A popular religious custom by which people assemble on set evenings, such as the 15th, 17th, 19th, and 23rd of January, May, and September, hold a religious ceremony, offer food to the deity, and pray. *Tsuki-machi,* meaning "waiting for the moon," refers to their waiting for the moon to appear.

Tsuki-nami no matsuri : A festival celebrated on set days each month (for example, on the first and fifteenth) in a shrine for thanksgiving and supplication.

Tsumi : In ordinary usage is no different in meaning from the English word "sin." However, in old Shinto, sickness, disaster, and error were also called *tsumi,* which was a most comprehensive concept. In antiquity a distinction was made between *Ama-tsu-tsumi* (Heavenly sins) and *Kuni-tsu-tsumi* (Terrestrial sins); *Ama-tsu-tsumi* were those which were committed by the god Susano-o-no-mikoto in Heaven and included destructive acts harming agriculture. *Kuni-tsu-tsumi* included inflicting injury or death, immodest actions, killing of domestic animals, using magic, leprosy, the falling of lightning, and damage done by harmful birds. By this one notices that the occurrence of evil was understood as being caused by something out of man's control; evil, including even moral and criminal offenses committed by man, was considered to be caused by the disturbances of the evil spirit Magatsuhi, who intruded from the land of Yomi. Therefore, salvation from *tsumi* was considered possible by *harae**, that is, by the removal of impediments, purification, and the the expulsion of the evil spirit Magatsuhi. This *harae,* as the return to a normal condition, was repeated day and night as a premise to divine worship. There is no idea of original sin in Shinto. On the contrary, it is believed that all sin and pollution can be removed by *harae.* This does not mean, however, that there is no acceptance of the responsibility for restitution for sin. The sinner is regarded, not as a born criminal, but as having been a member of a world of good and happiness; it is believed that by reminding him of this, the first step is taken to conquer evil and restore him from unhappiness, and that this is the basis for making him realize his responsibility as a child of the gods. There is a great historical difference in the idea of sin between antiquity and the present day; but the emphasis on *harae* is a constant religious attitude.

Tsutsushimi: A circumspect attitude; an attitude carefully obeying precepts and rules; an attitude careful not to be guilty of disrespect or failure. An attitude especially necessary when serving a god or a noble or when dealing with matters pertaining to a god or a noble. *Saikai** and religious ceremonies are performed with *tsutsushimi,* and the purification of sin or pollution is also connected with *tsutsushimi.* Yamazaki Ansai, the founder of Suiga Shintô, discovered a special significance in *tsutsushimi* and made it the basic principle of Shinto. *Tsutsushimi* is the same meaning as the " reverence " which was the basic morality of Neo-Confucianism; this was one of the momenta for syncretism between Shinto and Confucianism.

Tsûzoku Shintô: Vulgar Shinto, popular Shinto. From the outward meaning of the term, can be made to mean Shinto transformed into popular belief. But historically, refers to the Shinto of those who, basing themselves on Shinto faith, carried on simple, practical religious education and ethical education among the masses during the period of the Shinto revival of recent centuries, while the scholars of *Kokugaku,* basing themselves on study of the classics, exerted themselves in reviving an academic Shinto. Most of these people also popularized Buddhism and Confucianism and energetically incorporated their teachings. *Shingaku** was a movement of mass moral education which arose at this same period and can be called, in the broad sense, an example of popular Shinto. There are many ways in which popular Shinto is directly connected with the origin of the later sectarian Shinto movements.

Ubusuna-no-kami: The deity of the locality where one was born. The person belonging to an *ubusuna no kami** is called the *ubu-ko;* the newly born child is taken for a first visit to the shrine of the deity, who becomes the god protecting the person even after he reaches maturity and may move to another locality in which case he returns to his native village and participates in the festival of the *ubusuna no kami.* Originally, *ubusuna no kami* was a different concept from *uji-gami** and *chinju no kami*,* but they became confused in recent ages and it is no longer easy to distinguish between them. It is common for belief in *ubusuna no kami* to arise in social conditions where kin solidarity has broken down.

Uchimaki : ⟶ Sanku.

Ue no kinu : ⟶ Hô.

Uji-gami : Anciently referred to the deity worshipped as the ancestral or tutelary deity of a certain clan or family; since the middle ages has been thought of more frequently as the tutelary deity of one village. In Japan the migrations of clan communities have been complex, and there have been alterations in the meaning of *uji-gami* with time. At any rate, one of the central characteristics of Shrine Shinto is the prominence of the idea of ancestor worship accompanied by growing as consciousness of the *uji-gami* as common ancestor and by increasing solidarity with a spirit near to that of blood kinship.

Uji-ko : Innate believers or parishioners of a shrine living within the traditional parish boundaries of a shrine. Originally referred to the entire membership of a clan possessing common ancestral gods or *uji-gami**, but in later ages, the meaning changed, and *uji-gami* came to mean the god of persons living in a certain area; and those who were born and lived in the area and who were under the tuelage of the *uji-gami* came to be called *uji-ko*.

Uji-ko kai : An organization of *uji-ko** for the purpose of keeping up a shrine. Usually composed of all the inhabitants of the area in which the shrine is located. Governed by election from the membership of a committee and an *uji-ko sōdai,* or parishioner representatives.

Umi-no-kami : Literally, "god of the ocean." The deity ruling the seas; actually considered to be three deities called Wata-tsumi-no-kami. Popularly the dragon-god (*ryūjin*) is thought to be the god of the sea and is worshipped at a festival around June; there are many taboos on words and actions in order to avoid the anger of the sea-god while at sea.

Utsushi-yo : The actual world in which we live. Used in distinction to *Takama no Hara*, Tokoyo no kuni, Yomo-tsu-kuni*, Kakuri-yo**, etc. Originally is imperfect in comparison with *Takama no Hara,* but is a land conforming to the will of Amaterasu-ō-mikami and purified and consecrated for the performance of her worship; therefore it is also a land of religious hope, brightened with the light of prosperity, peace, and progress. The optimistic Shinto world view is based on this tenet.

Uyamau: A word also called *iyamau* in ancient Japanese. *Iya* means actions showing respect, etiquette or ceremonial behavior. Originally, *iyamau* meant to show respect by appropriate formal behavior, but today means also to respect internally. It is an attitude towards the gods, nobles, superiors, or superior personalities; and also a necessary attitude or state of mind in dealing mutually with relatives and friends. This concept is connected with the Shinto view of man. See *hito*.

Wagon: Sacred Japanese harp or *koto* played to *gagaku**.

Waka-miya: A type of shrine embodying the Shinto belief in "multiplying the spirit" of the deity enshrined. These shrines differ according to the beliefs of each shrine, but in generally they can be divided into three main groups: those which console the "divided spirit" of the god enshrined in the main shrine; those which console the "divided spirit" of the offspring of the main god; and those which console the revengeful spirit–the latter represents a fiercer form of the belief in "multiplying spirits."

Watarai, Nobuyoshi (1615–1691): A priest of the Grand Shrine of Ise, responsible for the development of later Ise Shinto. Rejecting Buddhist tendencies in Ise Shinto, he introduced Confucian elements and worked for the popularization of Shinto, closely relating religion and morality.

Yabusame.

Watarai Shintô: ⟶ Ise Shintô.

Wazawai: Disaster. In antiquity was regarded as a type of *tsumi** and was removed by *harae**. Since disaster is originally a type of *tsumi,* it is thought that in order to be restored to the society of those participating in religious rites as children of the gods, purification of body and mind was necessary. Besides this, there are many who think of *harae* as being a magic force to change disaster into a blessing.

Yabusame: A contest of shooting knob-headed arrows from a running horse at square wooden targets set up in three places. Performed by warriors since the late Heian period. Believed to be performed at shrine festivals because of its original significance as a means of divining whether the year's harvest would be plentiful.

Yama-boko : A float drawn around on festive occasions. The *yama-boko* draw around at the *Gion matsuri** of the Yasaka Jinja in Kyôto are particularly well known and are precious cultural treasures.

Yama-boko.

Yama-miya : "Mountain shrine." There are many cases, such as that of Sengen Jinja, where a mountain is the central feature of belief, of there being a *yama-miya* at the summit or on the mountainside, and of conducting processions and other religious ceremonies between the *yama-miya* and the *honsha**. There are cases where the *yama-miya* is considered as an interior shrine; but concerning its origins, there is a theory that the *yama-miya* may have been an old graveyard of the clan worshipping that shrine.

Yama-no-kami.

Yama-no-kami : Literally, "god of the mountains." There are two kinds: first, the god who governs the mountains; and second, the god of agricultural cultivation. The first type is worshipped by hunters, charcoal-burners, and woodcutters, and the deities enshrined are Ô-yama-tsumi-no-mikoto or Ko-no-hana-saku-ya-hime. There are many highly varied traditions connected with this worship, but the practice of offering the salt-sea fish called *okoze* is widespread. The second type is the same as the *ta no kami** worshipped by the peasantry and is thought to be a different god from the first type.

Yamato-mai : Literally, "Dance of Yamato." A dance believed to contain the spirit of the land of Yamato, the area around present-day Nara prefecture. During the Yamato period it was taken into the Court and performed at festivals such as *Daijô-sai** and *Chinkon-sai*. Also entered into a part of the *Kagura** songs. Various *Yamato-mai* songs were used at the festivals of the *Ise Jingû** and the various great shrines.

Yamazaki, Ansai (1618-1682): A Confucian scholar of the Chu Hsi school as well as Shinto scholar. Viewing the portion of the *Nihon Shoki* dealing with the age of the gods and the *Nakatomi no Ô-barae no Kotoba* as most important, he regarded *"tsutsushimi"* (discretion) as the fundamental principle in Shinto morality and founded *Suiga Shintô**. His followers were said to amount to over 6,000, and his teachings spread throughout the country.

Yashiki-gami.

Yashiki-gami: A deity enshrined in a corner of a dwelling house (*yashiki*). There are cases both where one exists in each house in a village and where one exists only in a definite influential house; the latter is considered to be the older form. In this case, there are cxamples of the *yashiki-gami* of the influential family becoming the tutelary deity of the entire village. The *yashiki-gami* has a deep connection with belief in ancestral spirits.

Yogoto: A kind of *norito**. A formula blessing and assuring that the reign of the Emperor will continue to flourish for ever. In the Shinto classics there exist such *yogoto* as the *Nakatomi no yogoto* pronounced on the day of the Emperor's ascension to the throne, and the *yogoto* pronounced at court by the ruler (*miyatsuko*) of the land of Izumo at the beginning of a new reign.

Yôhai-jo: In cases where the shrine which is the object of worship is located far away, and it is difficult to go there directly to worship, facilities necessary for worship, in other words, a *Haiden* (Oratory) is established and worship from afar (*yôhai*) is performed. The building where *yôhai* is performed is called *yôhai-jo*.

Yomi: The land where the dead go. The world where evil, unhappiness, destruction, curses, etc., originate. Whereas the gods of *Takama no Hara** bestow blessings; *Yomi* is inhabited by an evil spirit called Magatsuhi. Whereas *Takama no Hara* is the ideal world, *Yomi* is its antithesis.

Yori-shiro : ⟶ Shintai.

Yoshida, Kanetomo (1435-1511) : Founder of Yoshida Shintô (or Yuiitsu Sôgen Shintô). Author of the works *Shintô Tai-i* and *Yuiitsu Shintô Myôbô Yôshû*. Explaining the significance of Shinto by means of the Shinto theories handed down in the Yoshida family, he taught that Shinto was the basis of the three religions Confucianism, Buddhism, and Taoism. Noteworthy for his restoration of the ideological independence of Shinto.

Yoshida Shintô : One of the academic schools of Shintô. It is also called *Gempon Sôgen Shintô* (meaning Fundamental, Elemental Shinto), *Yuiitsu Shintô* (Only One Shinto), and *Urabe Shintô*. The Shinto learning which had beed handed down since the Heian period in the Yoshida family (anciently a family of diviners serving in the Court, later served as priests in the Yoshida Jinja and Hirano Jinja of Kyôto) was, in the medieval period, summarized, organized, and systematized by the hand of Yoshida Kanetomo* (1435–1511). It teaches the unity of Shinto, Buddhism, and Confucianism, with Shinto as the basic factor; although recognizing the external existence of *kami**, it also sees *kami* dwelling internally in the individual soul; and it emphasizes purity and cleanliness. From the later medieval period until the Meiji Restoration, this school of Shinto was propagated throughout the country and was influential in appointments to the priesthood and in decisions regarding religious ceremonies, etc.

Yudate : A ceremony in which water is boiled in a large cauldron on a coarse straw mat inside the shrine precincts and the hot water is sprinkled with bamboo leaves on themselves and the worshippers by the priests and *miko* ;* believed to signify the casting off of impurities by bathing in the sacred hot water. There are also cases when it is performed in order for the *miko* to utter trance prophecies. It is also widely performed as a musical ceremony called *yudate-kagura*.

Zen : Good. Besides good in the moral sense, also refers to happiness and superiority of the nature or value of a thing. In ancient Japan, effort began to be made to compile a list of virtues after the influence of Confucianism and Buddhist had been felt; since Confucianism and Buddhism were adapted to Japanese society, there never developed a branch of knowledge interested in making a list of virtues in native Japanese morality. However, this does not mean that good was not known and not practiced; there are scholars who explain that since actually moral standards were high, there was little need of moral teachings. Be that as it may, this must have something to do with the fact that in Shinto practice was demanded more than abstract knowledge, it was felt that, rather than being formalistic, it was better to act in conformity with the changes of actuality, and there was a consciousness that good was usual and evil extraordinary. At any rate, the good taught by Confucianism and Buddhism was accepted in the Shinto society and was practised diligently.

Zôka-no-sanshin : ⟶ Musubi.

INDEX

E

F

G

H

I

P

R

S

T

U

V

W

Y

ITEMIZED LIST OF TERMS

分 類 項 目 表

III. 神　名

IV. 神　社

v. 祭　祀

VI. 祭祀者

VII. 信仰集團

VIII. 雜の部